To Louis

From Ma — Love & Good Luck!

THINK LIKE A SHRINK

THINK LIKE A SHRINK

SOLVE YOUR PROBLEMS YOURSELF WITH SHORT-TERM THERAPY TECHNIQUES

CHRIST ZOIS, M.D.
WITH PATRICIA FOGARTY

WARNER BOOKS

A Time Warner Company

Copyright © 1992 by The Stonesong Press, Inc.,
Christ Zois, M.D., and Patricia Fogarty
All rights reserved
Warner Books, Inc., 666 Fifth Avenue, New York, NY 10103

Printed in the United States of America
First printing: February 1992

10 9 8 7 6 5 4 3 2 1

Produced by The Stonesong Press, Inc.

Library of Congress Cataloging-in-Publication Data
Zois, Christ.
    Think like a shrink : solve your problems yourself with short-term therapy
techniques / by Christ Zois, with Patricia Fogarty.
        p.   cm.
    Includes bibliographical references.
    ISBN 0-446-51647-3
    1. Brief psychotherapy—Popular works.   I. Fogarty, Patricia.
II. Title.
RC480.55.Z65   1992
616.89'14—dc20   91-50073
                                                                      CIP

Book Design by H. Roberts

To the memory of Peter Douvres, M.D., a
physician and friend who embodied the highest
ideals of service to others

A book must be the axe to shatter the frozen sea within us.

—Franz Kafka

Contents

INTRODUCTION / 1

PART I: Looking at Old Things in a New Way / 5

1: What Is Short-Term Therapy? / 7
2: Short-Term Therapy: Why It's Better / 47
3: Masks, Shields, and Cover-ups / 63
4: Your Buried Feelings: Hidden But
   Not Silenced / 89
5: The Traps Your Hidden Feelings Create / 115

PART II: The Defenses in Action: Understanding
   and Moving Past Them / 141

6: The Masks We Wear in Relationships / 149
7: Subverting Success at Work / 173
8: The Most Difficult Word: "Good-bye" / 189
9: Learning to Live without Defenses / 211
10: Mental Fitness / 243
ACKNOWLEDGMENTS / 255
BIBLIOGRAPHY / 257

THINK
LIKE A
SHRINK

Introduction

As a second-year resident in psychiatry, I saw a videotape of a twelve-session treatment of a patient. It wasn't short-term therapy; the patient and the therapist had simply agreed on twelve sessions, which were taped for teaching purposes. The approach was traditional and didn't involve a particular technique, although the therapist was verbal and responded actively to the patient.

For years afterward I thought about that videotape, which was the most significant learning tool I had encountered during my psychiatric residency. However, I was not yet aware of a technique that would allow for a complete therapy in a shorter period of time. As a result, for the next seven years I practiced an eclectic type of long-term therapy: I relied on traditional concepts but was more active than passive in responding to patients.

Then I saw videotapes of short-term therapy sessions that changed my way of thinking. For the first time I was exposed to work intended as short-term treatment. It was not long-term therapy cut short. This was therapy that made use of an effective technique that could accomplish as much as long-term therapy, if not more, but in a brief period of time. I immediately became involved in short-term work and have never looked back.

Brilliance is the ability to look at old things in a new way. Our mind-sets are clusters of interacting ideas, emotions, and attitudes that color our observations. These clusters—some people call them their philosophies of life—give rise to expectations that we tend to fulfill; meanwhile, however, our objectivity is diminished greatly by their emotional and subjective quality. Allowing un-examined mind-sets to determine our attitudes and actions can result in mental stagnation, which is often manifested as arrogance and inflexibility or, worse, as maladaptive or self-defeating behavior.

Accepting that short-term therapy works requires a willingness to put old beliefs in abeyance. In my own work, I always hope to do things differently tomorrow in light of what I learn today.

How accurate are your perceptions about psychotherapy? Answer the following ten questions—true or false—and check your responses against mine. Full explanations are given in the chapters that follow.

1. Traditional long-term therapists use a proven technique in helping patients.
2. Short-term therapy works on the deepest level of the unconscious.
3. Short-term therapy is used mainly for crisis intervention.
4. A therapy that lasts eight years provides longer-lasting results than one that lasts eight months.
5. Confidentiality is a valuable and helpful element in psychotherapy.
6. If the patient doesn't want to discuss a certain topic, the therapist should respect the patient's wishes.

7. Freud handed down an effective technique to succeeding generations of therapists.
8. Therapists must treat most of their patients with delicacy, since they are in a fragile state.
9. To grow emotionally, we must face the worst things about ourselves.
10. Therapists should give their patients advice.

1. false	6. false
2. true	7. false
3. false	8. false
4. false	9. true
5. false	10. false

As you read this book, your ideas about psychotherapy—everything from what a patient should derive from the first day of therapy to the idea of being "cured"—are likely to undergo significant modification.

Think like a Shrink explains the universal issues that everyone confronts and helps you understand how you have responded to them. In addition, the book offers a base of knowledge about what to expect from a therapist. If you're in therapy—short-term or not—or planning to be, after you've read this volume you will understand the elements that make up an effective therapy.

Chapter 1 explains the short-term technique. I will take you step by step through verbatim dialogue from an actual therapy session. My direct comments on the interaction between therapist and patient begin to show you how to think like a shrink. Chapter 2 discusses short-term therapy within the context of psychotherapy in general, exploring issues surrounding short-term therapy and making the case that it is a preferable mode of treatment.

Chapter 3 explains the defenses, the attitudes, and ways

of behaving that shield us from our problems: You'll learn what they are and how they operate in your life. Chapters 4 and 5 take you deep within the human psyche (the complex of thoughts, emotions, memories, and attitudes that shape our perceptions and compel our behavior) below the defenses— to the "core" feelings that the defenses hide.

Chapters 6, 7, and 8, which synthesize the information presented in the earlier chapters, present nine case studies— again with verbatim dialogue—that highlight the problems people encounter in relationships, at work, and when they suffer a loss. As you read actual dialogue and my explanations of therapeutic responses and interpretations, you are once again in the mind of the working therapist. Seeing the ways in which I help patients break through their defenses to resolve their problems can give you insight into your own attitudes, emotions, and ways of behaving.

Chapters 9 and 10 elaborate on the work you can do in facing the painful issues in your life. By striving for a clear perspective on your problems and a balanced view of your relationships with others, you can achieve the intimacy with other people that is essential for a sense of harmony with your world.

PART I

Looking at Old Things in a New Way

CHAPTER 1

What Is Short-Term Therapy?

"When was the last time you saw your father?"

"The night he died."

"What did you say to him then?"

"He had been feeling bad, and he wanted to go to the hospital. There was a screwup in getting him a hospital bed, and my mother and I got into an argument about what happened. She was saying it was my fault we didn't get him in, and I was saying it was her fault. And he yells, 'Shut up.'"

"Who did he yell at?"

"At me. I didn't say anything. I was sitting in the kitchen; he was in the family room. I just kept eating. We had the argument and all. But then I didn't go over and kiss him when I said good night, which was something I'd started doing in the recent past and which he really liked. I didn't go over and kiss him, and then he died that night."

"What was your thought when you didn't go over and kiss him?"

"That he rejected me, because he had yelled at me."

"How were you feeling toward him at that moment?"

"I felt that he yelled at me because he was on medication and very ill."

"You rationalize that it was the medication and his illness that caused him to yell at you, but still you didn't go kiss him."

"No."

"So how were you feeling toward him?"

"I guess I was angry that he yelled at me."

"You say 'I guess.'"

"I was angry with him."

"When you left to go home, what did you say to him?"

"Good night."

When the man got home, his mother called to say his father was having a heart attack. By the time he returned to his parents' home, his father was dead.

"What was the funeral like?"

The man pauses. "It was terrible."

"You say it was terrible. What was terrible about it?"

He pauses a long while. "I can't talk about that."

"How do you feel right now?"

"Distraught."

"Have you thought about the funeral before?"

"Yes."

"Have you ever discussed this with anybody?"

"No." His eyes fill with tears.

"So you've kept your feelings locked up."

"Yes."

"Have you cried about it when you were alone?"

"Yes."

"What was terrible about that day?"

"He was dead."

"What were your thoughts about that?"

He pauses a long while. He stares at his hands, and his eyes fill with tears again. "I had failed to keep him alive."

*   *   *

This transcription of a videotaped short-term therapy session illustrates how we tend to bury negative thoughts and emotions. Unfortunately, burying such memories and feelings keeps us from a sense of well-being and harmony with our world. Despite our attempts to ignore them, these issues continue to exist, below the level of our everyday awareness, cheating us of our resources and diminishing our productivity.

The technique used in analytically oriented short-term therapy quickly and effectively gets to that level. The short-term therapist actively works to help patients confront and resolve their most difficult problems. As you read this book, you will learn how to put the concepts and techniques of short-term therapy to work in your own life.

Classic passive approaches to psychotherapy are contrary to a medical approach to problem-solving. A surgeon doesn't say, "The abscess we discovered in your abdomen took twelve months to develop, so we'll have to work on it for at least six to twelve months." After an initial diagnosis, the short-term therapist takes steps to cure the condition, using techniques that aggressively seek to solve the problem and taking only as much time as is necessary. A short-term therapy can take from several weeks to eight or ten months.

Medical science has assumed a position of great power and authority, and yet, when it comes to therapy for emotional ills, for decades we have put up with an approach that ignores the medical model of treatment.

Short-term therapy returns to the medical model by stressing technique and a clear beginning, middle, and end. The therapist first assesses your psychological makeup and the problem areas in your life and develops a strategy for treating them; then he or she applies the short-term technique to overcome your defenses and address your core issues, allowing you to take an inventory of your emotions and work through them until finally the treatment is complete.

The Initial Evaluation—Mapping Out the Treatment

In the initial evaluation, the short-term therapist examines with you the universal issues that are fundamental to your existence: the ability to act on your own behalf versus self-sabotage; dependence versus independence; inappropriate attachment to another person versus the ability to say good-bye; action versus passivity; the ability to tolerate loss versus chronic grieving; emotional isolation versus the ability to experience your feelings; distancing versus intimacy.

Those who set out to improve their quality of life must scrutinize these issues; they are essential to understanding the dynamics of an individual's psyche. Listed below are some of the questions I ask in order to elicit the ways in which these universal issues manifest themselves in a patient's life.

You can simply read over these questions in order to learn about the material covered in an initial evaluation. However, taking a few moments to carefully consider your personal responses will increase both your self-awareness and your appreciation of the material this book presents. As you proceed through these chapters, you may find yourself modifying your responses and reassessing your reactions to the questions. That modification and reassessment is what I had in mind in writing this book.

This list is a bare-bones overview of the information that I elicit in an evaluation. As you read further, you'll observe the technique that therapists use to help their patients unearth buried conflicts, feelings, and impulses.

- *How would you describe yourself?*

    In general, do you consider yourself a happy, satisfied person or an unhappy person?

    What do you consider your problems to be today?

- *Do you feel anger about people or situations in your past or present life?*
- *Do you see yourself as a passive or an active person?*
- *Do you have feelings of guilt about people or events in your past or present life?*
- *What is or was your relationship with your parents?*

    Which parent are you or were you closer to?

    What was your relationship with your parents while you were growing up?

    Has that relationship changed? What is it today?

    What was your knowledge of their relationship to each other, both emotional and physical? Did you have evidence they were having sex? How did you react to that?

    Have you discussed with your parents your relationship and your feelings about them, both negative and positive?

    Are you prepared to say good-bye to your parents?

    What will you miss about them when they die?

    If one or both of your parents have died, what was it like when you said good-bye for the last time? Can you discuss that event today without pain or sorrow? Are your memories of them positive or negative? What do you miss about them?

- *What is your relationship with your siblings?*

    What was your relationship when you were growing up?

    Has that relationship changed? What is it today?

    Have you discussed with your siblings your relationship and your feelings about them, both negative and positive?

- *Did any other significant people live in your household? What was your relationship to them?*
- *Do you have a satisfying sex life?*

    What contributes to that satisfaction or lack of satisfaction?

When did you first have sexual fantasies? What
were they?
When did you first masturbate?
When did you first have intercourse?
What are your fantasies when you masturbate? When
you have intercourse? Is there a recurring fantasy?
Is there more than one other person in your fantasy?

- *Do you consider your current relationships with lovers, spouses,
  friends, and children more positive than negative or more
  negative than positive?*
- *What are your relationships with co-workers, superiors,
  subordinates? What are your feelings toward them?*
- *Are you satisfied with your career?*
  Do you consider yourself successful?
  Are you happy or unhappy with your work?
  If you're unhappy, why?
- *How would you feel about losing specific people in your life?*
  How would you react?
  What would you miss about them?
  What would you remember?
  What wouldn't you miss?

Two key dynamics of the short-term therapy technique
will come into play as you ask and answer these questions.
First, the questions generate defenses that are designed to
hide some of the painful material the questions evoke.
During an evaluation, as indeed throughout therapy, when
resistance comes up in the form of a defense, I stop asking
questions and immediately challenge the defense. If I didn't
do that, any "information" I gained and any "insight" the
patient developed would be meaningless.

The second dynamic concerns emotions that emerge
when the defenses are challenged. In short-term therapy,
therapist and patient examine these emotions, link them
with past emotions surrounding a recalled event, and then
deal with, or work through, them. As this process takes

place, emotions that in the past were formidable become less threatening; they become modified and manageable in the present and for the future.

In addition to eliciting information about these key issues in your life, the initial evaluation, which can take an hour or several hours, sets the tone of the relationship between therapist and patient. This session has to accomplish many things for the therapist. It must:

- Provide a clear picture of the major issues in the patient's life
- Allow the therapist to assess the patient's defenses, which the therapist challenges from the outset
- Let the therapist assess the size of the gap between the patient's thoughts and feelings
- Enable the therapist to relate the patient's problems to past and current issues, so that the patient can experience in the present emotions he* has buried
- Provide opportunities for intimacy between therapist and patient during which the patient shows emotion
- Generate enough information so that the therapist can develop a strategy
- Enable the therapist to estimate how many sessions the treatment will require

The information generated in the initial evaluation is shared with the patient as the therapist clarifies and elaborates on the patient's perception of his problems. At the end of the session the patient has some knowledge about the disturbances in his life and where they have come from, how he has used defenses instead of facing those problems, and some understanding of what he has to do to resolve them.

In a way that is explicit and clear, in the course of the initial evaluation the patient acknowledges, for example, his

---

*To avoid repeating the awkward construction "he or she" and its permutations, the masculine pronoun is used when the general sense of "person" is intended.

anger and guilt and self-destructiveness. He becomes aware that a difficulty he came in with—a bad relationship with his wife or a chronic problem on his job—is not an isolated matter but part of a complex series of issues and that he has contributed to the difficulty that he perceives.

After the initial evaluation, the therapist should be able to understand what is wrong with the patient, what can be done about it, and how long it's going to take. (That sounds simple and straightforward enough, but within the therapeutic establishment it's still considered heretical.)

There is nothing mystical or magical about making an assessment. Effective therapists do this in a straightforward way. They simply have to know what to look for and, depending on what they find, be able to understand how much there is to do. A key part of making a diagnosis is evaluating the individual's level of defensiveness, the types of defenses he or she uses, and the patient's capacity to distinguish defenses from authentic emotions. Therapy for someone who readily identifies and easily acknowledges emotions will not take as long as the treatment of a person who has a great deal of difficulty owning up to unpleasant or painful emotions.

To illustrate what takes place in an initial evaluation as well as the principal elements of the short-term technique, I've chosen the case of Charles,* a thirty-two-year-old man who entered therapy because in almost all areas of his life he was unable to accomplish anything significant. A college graduate with a degree in physics, he worked as a carpenter's assistant. Although he was very bright and had won a scholarship to a leading graduate school, he had not entered a degree program. He was unable to sustain personal relationships.

---

*Throughout the book, I have changed the names of patients and the people they mention. For economy and ease of expression, I use fictitious first names in the text. When I treat patients, however, I address them as Ms., Mrs., or Mr. and use the last name.

The dialogue that forms a large part of this chapter is a verbatim transcription of my evaluation of Charles. The dialogue has been taken directly from the videotape and has been edited only to protect the patient's identity and to reduce the material to a manageable length; this is not a complete transcription of the ninety-minute session, but the segments are given in the sequence in which they occurred.

By the end of this first session, I had determined that Charles's therapy would have to address several issues, including his extreme passivity; his paralysis in the face of his emotions, especially negative ones; and his inability to achieve intimacy, which had resulted in a series of failed relationships. It was clear that his self-destructive behavior and feelings of lack of entitlement stemmed from overwhelming guilt. Charles's defenses were ingrained and visible: he did a great deal of rationalizing, and he took a helpless, passive position throughout a large part of the evaluation.

I predicted that Charles's therapy would take forty sessions. This relatively lengthy estimate was based on his inability to deal with his emotions and the gap that existed between his thoughts and his feelings. One good sign was his ability to show emotion during the session; he allowed himself to be intimate with me by showing me his feelings. Charles completed his therapy in thirty-two sessions.

Principal Elements of the Short-Term Technique

Short-term therapy is similar to other talk therapies in that it is based on analytical concepts, but it is different in its approach—that is, in the activity of the therapist. Whereas most traditional therapists take a passive role and let the patient set the pace of the treatment, the short-term therapist employs active strategies that allow for resolution of the patient's problems within a short period of time.

Clarifying Feelings and Issues

A good therapy elicits clarity. Many people who enter treatment are vague about their problems. This difficulty is compounded by the ambiguity of everyday language: we all use the words "maybe," "perhaps," "I think," "I guess." Outside of therapy, this vagueness is tolerated and not questioned. As a result, most patients initially have difficulty describing their thoughts and feelings accurately.

Short-term therapists do not permit vagueness, which is one of the most common defenses. In a methodical way, we insist that patients commit and assert themselves. The therapist who tolerates vagueness is not going to help patients understand their problems; in allowing vagueness to pass unchallenged the therapist actually encourages a lack of progress.

The therapist must address a lack of clarity every time it occurs, until the patient sharpens his thought process and becomes aware of the need to be clear and committed in every statement made. "I think I am angry" is not acceptable. You are or you are not, and you must commit yourself one way or the other.

What follows is verbatim dialogue from my evaluation session with Charles, beginning a few minutes into the session. Charles and I discuss Dr. Frank (not her real name), a colleague in training at the institute where the sessions were held. Charles had seen her for an entry interview the previous week.

Zois: And what's your feeling right now? You said there was apprehension.

Charles: That I very much want to get on with this.

Zois: That's a description of what you want to accomplish. But you say you're apprehensive also. How do you experience that?

Charles: In a certain kind of nervousness.

Zois: How do you experience that nervousness?

Charles: I'm sweating a little bit.

Zois: In your mind, what's it like, the nervousness?

Charles: It's kind of free-floating.

Zois: What do you mean?

Charles: On the one hand, I feel that this is going to benefit me. I'm confident I want to go through with it....

Zois: That's one thought, but you're also nervous here with me, you say.

Charles: Yet at the same time a little apprehensive about what's going to go on.

Zois: So in your mind, here with me, what are you nervous about?

Charles: Um, just exactly what's going to unfold. I felt a little defensive last week, like I didn't have my feet on the ground.

Zois: You were defensive with Dr. Frank.

Charles: Not with her, just with...

Zois Well, who else was there?

Charles: It wasn't a defensiveness against her, just a defensiveness against the situation.

Zois: So you're putting it on the situation, but in terms of people, who was there?

Charles: It was myself.

Zois: You were alone?

Charles: No, but it wasn't directed toward her.

Zois: But if you say you were defensive, who were you defensive toward?

Charles: It was against myself.

Zois: You want to put it on yourself, but when you talk about being defensive, it implies that there was somebody there to be defensive toward. So who was there besides Dr. Frank?

Charles: (With mild irritation) Obviously no one else.

Zois: So it was Dr. Frank you were defensive against. Now
here, with me, do you feel that way?
Charles: No, not particularly.
Zois: You say, "Not particularly"—you do or you don't.
Charles: I'm ambivalent.
Zois: You're sitting on the fence.
Charles: That's what I just said.
Zois: But what about that? You're having some difficulty
taking a position with me.
Charles: Not with you per se.
Zois: But who else is here?

Charles reveals a lot about his psychological makeup in this
initial interaction. It's immediately obvious that he has great
difficulty declaring irritation or anger; he's unable to discuss
his negative feelings about Dr. Frank, who is not present. He
even admits to being vague and ambivalent. My comments are
designed to force him to be clear.

Challenging the Defenses

In the face of resistance, the exchange of information
between patient and therapist is meaningless. Because even
the most motivated patients come to treatment with some
degree of resistance, challenging it is a recurring component
of every therapy. Resistance manifests itself as a series of
defenses, which vary from person to person.

The short-term technique cuts through the smoke screen
of defenses the individual uses to obscure issues. The therapist focuses on the defenses and wears them down, in a
process that probes for the negative memories, emotions,
and impulses that are the source of our pain and unhappiness.

It's a straightforward situation: if you, as the patient, are
not answering the question, you are being defensive. As your
therapist, I must challenge your defenses immediately. We
have nothing to gain by waiting.

The challenge to your defenses arouses your anger, because I do not allow you to use your customary defenses, and I thus threaten to expose you to the painful feelings you have been trying to avoid. My questions also arouse your anxiety. You see that I am trying to get close to you emotionally, and your anxiety erupts because of the conflicts (painful, unresolved emotional issues) that emotional closeness can trigger. As I persist, however, your defenses are exhausted, and you feel relief as your blocked feelings begin to be liberated. The challenge to your defenses is the first step toward intimacy with the therapist, a key component of short-term therapy.

In my session with Charles, I try to help him clarify the emotion he felt with Dr. Frank. One result is his acknowledgment that he gets anxious when he's angry, and that he is feeling anxious now.

Zois: So when you get angry it makes you anxious.

Charles: Yes.

Zois: And you have anxiety in declaring your anger toward me.

Charles: Yes, that's right.

Zois: So as we look at it here, how angry are you?

Charles: I don't know how to qualify the degree of it. It's a frustration in not being able to deal with the situation.

Zois: But you're angry with me. So what comes to your mind when you think of how angry you are?

Charles: Nothing, it's a blank. It's just a feeling of frustration. [This is the defense of *avoidance*—he tries to stay away from the emotion.*]

Zois: But, you see, now you want to move from anger to

---

*In the dialogues throughout the book, I have noted the defenses as they occur. In this chapter, I've provided only a few such comments. I'll discuss the most common defenses in full in Chapter 3.

frustration, and you tell me that your anger makes you anxious, so you want to get away from it. But if we were to look at it, how angry are you with me?

Charles: I don't know how to say it. [This is the defense of *helplessness*—passivity in the face of a challenge.]

Zois: Now you take a helpless position here. You're feeling angry, you're anxious, so you become helpless and passive. Is that familiar to you?

Charles: Yes, it is.

Zois: What comes to your mind?

Charles: That it's a cyclical situation.

Zois: That you become angry, it makes you anxious, and then you become passive in the face of it, with whomever you're angry at.

In a common short-term maneuver, I point out to Charles that his anger causes anxiety and that he then takes a defensive posture (his passivity) to quell his anxiety and to cover up his disturbing emotion. The anger I'm trying to get him to acknowledge is buried under layers of anxiety and defensiveness. The process of focusing, probing, and challenging is akin to working at an archaeological dig; the therapist must penetrate several strata—anxiety, passivity, and other defenses—before arriving at the core—in this case, the information Charles needs in order to make changes in his life.

Charles: But it's not so total. It's not always that way with all people and in all situations. [He is using the defense of *intellectualization*—analyzing or philosophizing about a difficult situation rather than facing it.]

Zois: You want to divide it up. But it's that way here with me now.

Charles: Yes, it is.

Zois: Is it that way with anybody else?

Charles: In particular with my family.

Zois: Who comes to mind in your family?

Charles: My brother does.

Once the patient has experienced the emotion with the therapist, the therapist attempts to link these feelings with significant people in the patient's life. Charles experiences anger and anxiety and is able to state that he has similar feelings when he deals with his brother.

Zois: Can you give me an illustration of when you've gotten angry with him and dealt with him the way you've dealt with me, becoming anxious and passive?

Charles: Well, the most recent event was a family dinner. My brother commented that he didn't like the fact that there were foreigners in the country because they were screwing it up, taking jobs away from hardworking Americans. I just said that they seemed to be well qualified for many jobs and were very hardworking and strived to get university educations and to enter the workplace in the best possible way. I then said, "It's better than being a bagger in a supermarket."

Zois: So then what happened?

Charles: His wife is a cashier in a supermarket. When I made that comment, she took it personally, hung out for fifteen minutes, and then left. He didn't say anything, but pretty soon he left, and I got the feeling they were pretty angry.

Zois: You knew why they were angry?

Charles: Yeah, sure, I figured it out, but I thought it was unjustified because it wasn't a personal slur. [This is the defense of *rationalization*—making excuses.]

Zois: So when he said this about the foreigners in the country, how were you feeling toward him?

Charles: That it was a pretty typical situation with him.

Zois: Again that is a description. What was your emotion toward him?

Charles: Just that he's an idiot.

Zois: That's another description. How do you feel toward him, that in your mind he's an idiot?

Charles: Well, it was one of resignation, I think.

Zois: But we see that you weren't resigned at all. You made a personal slur against his wife. So you weren't resigned at all.

Charles: But it wasn't a slur against his wife.

Zois: But who's a cashier?

Charles: But it was against the mindless worker. I didn't say that all people who work in supermarkets are worthless.

Zois: But that's how she took it, and you knew she took it that way.

Charles: Yes, but it wasn't a personal slur.

Zois: But, you see, right now you tell yourself that it wasn't a personal slur, but she got angry and left and he did, too, and you knew why.

Charles: Right.

Zois: So did you slur her work because of your feelings toward your brother?

Charles: No. [He uses the defense of *denial*—exactly what the word says.]

Zois: You say no, but what were your feelings toward your brother? You say he's an idiot. You don't like what he says.

Charles: But I wouldn't attack his wife.

Zois: But you did.

Charles: But I didn't.

Zois: Well, we can discuss it all day here, but the truth is, as you describe it, you said something derogatory that his wife took personally. Now you say there's no relation between what you said about her and how you felt toward him.

Charles: I didn't piece it together, but maybe...

Zois: Well, as we look at it now...

Charles: Perhaps you're right. [The defense of *vagueness*—lack of focus and commitment to a feeling.]

Zois: You say "perhaps," but what do you say here, as you look at it? Number one, you haven't told me, how did you feel toward him when he said what he said about foreigners?

Charles is a resistant individual who has great difficulty acknowledging his emotions, even to himself and even though he can describe them. On the one hand, he says he's angry; on the other, he can't make the connection between the anger and his behavior with his brother and his wife. I stay with Charles's defenses in an attempt to get him to acknowledge, not only to me but to himself, what actually was going on in the conversation he describes.

Charles has difficulty declaring negative feelings; he becomes very anxious when they are discussed. I am attempting to ease that anxiety and facilitate his ability to describe these emotions with me. I want him eventually to be able to describe an emotion, such as anger, that he feels toward me—not only to announce it but to examine it as it occurs. Expressing his anger toward me will form the groundwork for his ability to describe deeper feelings of anger he may have had toward significant people in the past and present.

Defenses are often ingrained habits that are eradicated only with repeated effort. In challenging the defenses, repetition is important. The patient may see that an attitude is defensive or he may have an insight about his behavior, but that doesn't mean the defense goes away immediately or that the insight stays with him from that time onward. If you want to change, you have to keep rethinking the elements of your newly found awareness. You must experience them over and over until they become second nature.

Closing the Gap between Thought and Feeling

Some people are more in touch with their feelings than others. On one end of the spectrum are those who are aware of their feelings, are not intimidated by them, and can declare them; as a result they usually don't experience a sense of paralysis in their lives and don't have a lot of conflicts. Such people recognize the difference between an emotion and a defense; they don't say, "I was so angry I cried" or "I was so angry I left the room." They have no trouble expressing how they feel about the therapist and about other people. A short-term therapist can evaluate these patients and see within ten or fifteen minutes that they are pretty much in touch with their emotions.

Other people readily use defenses but are quick to learn not to. The therapist helps educate them about the difference between a defense and an emotion. These patients understand rather easily and by the end of the evaluation have changed some of their ways of responding. They no longer say "maybe," "I think," "I guess," and they take this new sense of clarity away with them.

At the far end of the spectrum are those people who are "in isolation," meaning that their thoughts and feelings are not in sync but operate on tracks that are far apart. Rather than admit irritation because of criticism leveled at them at work, they might say that the boss has been under a lot of stress. Such people often don't know what a feeling is. The result is emotional paralysis and very likely a failure to find success or contentment in life. This is the group to which Charles belonged.

By pressuring and challenging and focusing, the short-term therapist prompts these emotionally isolated patients to bring their thoughts and feelings together: "What do you mean?"..."You're describing what you did, not what you felt"..."What is your emotion?" The therapist keeps these patients boxed in and stays right on top of them so that they're up against the ropes. Finally their emotion emerges.

Therapists can allow less defensive individuals more latitude, but if constant pressure is not applied with highly resistant people like Charles, they will inevitably slip away into their defenses.

This dialogue immediately followed the one above.

Zois: You say "perhaps," but what do you say here, as you look at it? Number one, you haven't told me, how did you feel toward your brother when he said it?

Charles: That he's...

Zois: That's a description. What was your emotion toward him? What was your emotion toward your brother when he said that? [Once I hear a description rather than an emotion, I cut off the reply to maintain the pressure at as high a level as possible.]

Charles: That once again he's pulling the same old shit.

Zois: That's another description. How did you feel that he was pulling the same old shit?

Charles: I guess...

Zois: I guess?

Charles: I'm not really sure.

Zois: And now you're helpless here with me. Now you're smiling.

Charles: I go through family situations like that....

Zois: But here's one situation and you're having difficulty telling me your emotions with your brother. So now, if you were to look at it, what was it?

Charles: It was indifference, I suppose, more than anything else.

Zois: Indifference is not a feeling. You say, "I suppose" —so do you want to stay here sitting on the fence with me, or do you want to look at the situation and answer the question? I mean, if you sit here and straddle the fence and take a very ambivalent attitude about how you felt and how you feel, what's going to happen here?

Charles: Nothing's going to be gained from it, I know.

Zois: So why do you want to do that?

Charles: I don't want to. It's...

Zois You say, "I don't want to," but we see that there's a part of you that's committed to it, that there's a part of you that's going to defeat this process if you sit here and generalize and ruminate, and it will be like the rest of your life as you described it to Dr. Frank.

Charles: I don't know that it's hatred directed toward him, but it's hostility and...

Zois: But hatred comes to your mind.

Charles is an angry man, but he doesn't know how angry he is. Not only is he very resistant; he also suffers from a schism between his thoughts and his emotions. Having penetrated some of his defenses and entered into his psyche to some degree, I now appeal to the part of Charles that wants to change.

I've gotten the door open a crack and I shout in. What do I get back? A very loaded emotional word: "hatred." I do not introduce that word; it comes from him.

Charles: But I don't think it's that extreme.

Zois: But "I don't think" doesn't help us. The word "hate" comes to your mind toward him, so if you would be honest with yourself...

Charles: But it's not as extreme as that.

Zois: But that word comes to your mind.

Charles: Yes.

When the patient makes a statement of denial but uses a loaded word, I ignore the denial and instead focus on the word. I state to the patient that it is what has come to his mind. Of all the things he might have denied, why did he choose this word? Because it has significance for him.

Zois: Now, in that time, when you were sitting in that backyard, did you feel hate toward him?

Charles: Probably. There was—

Zois: "Probably" doesn't help you. You did or you didn't.

Charles: Yes, I did.

Zois: What did you see in your mind at that moment?

Charles: I'm not skirting the issue, but it also deals with my stepfather...

Zois: But you *are* skirting the issue. We'll get to your stepfather. But right at that moment, what did you see in your mind as you felt hate toward your brother?

Charles: That it's the same old shit.

Zois: All right, so you're looking at him, and how did you experience the hate?

Charles: You mean how did I perceive it?

Zois: Yes.

Charles Through indifference.

Zois: But you see, you have this very angry feeling toward him, which you identify to the point of hating him, and then you rationalize away from that feeling by citing indifference, which isn't a feeling. But at that moment you tell me that you felt hate for him. And then you stuffed that feeling. You didn't declare your anger toward him. But instead you made some general comment about his wife. [With a further instructive comment, I again point out to Charles how he deals with his anger—by failing to acknowledge it even to himself.]

Charles: So I just defused it and put it on her.

Zois: You put it on her. So then she leaves and he leaves. But you have a lot of anxiety about your anger, so you deny to yourself that you took your rage toward him and put it on her, and that the comment was in fact directed at her and you knew it was. But you have a lot of difficulty acknowledging that impulse to get at him through her.

Charles: You're right. I never saw it that way before, that's all. Not this situation, anyway.

Zois: As you look at it now, is there validity to what I'm saying?

Charles: Yes, there is.

Reaching Buried Emotions

The work of the session so far has been geared to getting past the defenses to reach Charles's buried emotions. At this point I need to address another issue that has not surfaced but that might be contributing to Charles's resistance with me. At the beginning of the session, he had mentioned his surprise that Dr. Frank was not going to see him that day. His comment was significant because, at the end of Dr. Frank's session with him, she had told him I would do the next evaluation.

Zois: How did you feel that I came between you and Dr. Frank?

Charles: I don't know that I want to answer the question about you coming between us. It's not like it's anything more than just the continuity of seeing the same person again.

Zois: In your mind you say there's something more to it?

Charles: No, you said "come between us," as if...

Zois: I'm here, she's not.

Charles: Yes, right.

Zois: So you said there's something more to that.

Charles: No, I said when you said—

Zois: Well, who said what, but it's what's on your mind. We're clear on what I said, right? Now you're smiling. How do you feel right now here?

Charles: Absolutely foolish.

Zois: You feel foolish? Why do you feel foolish?

Charles: It seems that whatever I say, it doesn't seem to cover what you want, and I just feel, uh...

Zois: How do you feel toward me?

Charles: That you're the master and I'm the child.

Zois: What does that feel like?

Charles: It feels stupid. I feel stupid.

Zois: You feel stupid. What's the emotion that goes along with that?

Charles: It's just being put in a secondary position—

Zois: What's the emotion that you feel here, being, in your mind, in that position with me?

Charles: Not useless, but kind of...

Zois: What's the emotion?

Charles: I guess one of being left out.

Zois: You say, "I guess" left out, but that's not an emotion. How do you feel toward me here that you describe me as the master, you the child, you in a subordinate position, you secondary. You must have a lot of feelings that that's going on.

Charles: Well, I don't like that position.

Zois: Well, how do you feel toward me, that I'm putting you in that position in your mind?

Charles: That it's nothing that I can change, but I'd like equality.

Zois: But, you see, you're still intellectualizing. I still don't know how you feel toward me here at this minute.

Charles: I'm not sure how I feel.

Zois: Now again you're going to a passive position, sitting on the fence, but your descriptions are very precise—that you're here in a subordinate position, that I'm the master and you're the child. So what's the emotion that goes along with that?

Charles: Just one of being subjugated...

Zois: That's more description. What's your feeling?

Charles: I guess, it's—

Zois: Again, "I guess."

Charles: A certain anger.

Zois: So you're angry with me.

Charles: I guess so.

Zois: You say, "I guess so."

Charles: Yes.

Zois: You are. How angry are you?

Charles: I'm not going to attack you or anything.

Zois: You had that thought, though.

Through this interchange Charles comes to a description and discussion of his anger with me. Part of that anger stems from his perception that I had replaced Dr. Frank. The thought of someone coming between him and another person is tied to other relationships in his life, and he now transfers it onto me. Another part of his anger arises from my probing into his inner life. (Probing generates irritation as a natural concomitant of all treatment.) Charles's acknowledgment of his anger toward me allows him for the first time to look in a meaningful way at his anger toward the significant people in his life.

I continue to question Charles about how he would like to attack me, reassuring him that this is a fantasy. Our dialogue moves to the issue of violence, which he says he experienced when he was growing up. The person who comes to his mind is his stepfather, who verbally and physically abused both him and his mother. The incident Charles describes took place when he was sixteen.

Charles: One night I just couldn't take it anymore. It was late at night, and I went in and broke up a fight, and he turned on me, and I fought back.

Zois: He was striking your mother?

Charles: Yes.

Zois: With his fists?

Charles: Yes.

Zois: And where was he hitting her?

Charles: At the point I came in he was just hitting her, he was sitting down. They had twin beds; he was sitting across from her.

Zois: She was sitting on her bed?

Charles: Yes, she was sitting on her bed.

Zois: And he was sitting on his bed across from her, and lashing out at her with his fists.

Charles: He was clothed, and she was in a nightgown.

Zois: And where were his punches landing?

Charles: Just her upper torso.

Zois: And where were you when you heard this?

Charles: In the bedroom that I shared with my brother.

Zois: So you went in, and then what happened? You say he turned on you.

Charles: Yeah, I don't know that I attacked him. I think I said something to him, and then he came after me.

Zois: He got up.

Charles: He got up and came after me.

Zois: And then he tried to punch you?

Charles: And the next thing I remember we were—

Zois: He tried to punch you?

Charles: Yeah, and we were out of the bedroom and in the living room somewhere and fighting and—

Zois: What were you doing? Were you punching him back?

Charles: More than anything else, I was dancing around, and trying to avoid having to hit him.

Zois: You were trying to avoid having to hit him.

Charles: But I remember at one point knocking him down.

Zois: How'd you do that?

Charles: Well, his balance wasn't great, even though he was much stronger than I was, and I wasn't going to take a punch for the hell of it, so I just knocked him off balance.

Zois: How'd you do it? How'd you knock him off balance?

Charles: I was on the wrestling team, so I just saw where he was weakest, and I just dove into his legs and knocked him on his ass, scissored him.

Zois: Cut his legs out from under him and he fell down? Then what happened?

Charles: I don't know exactly, but this went on for a long enough time that it exhausted him, and at some point I remember saying that I'd had enough of this, I'm going to call the cops. And he said something about I didn't have the balls to do it, so I called the cops. The cops came and they were friends of his, and they were horrified to see that he would do this, and he was completely mortified. The cops were there for maybe twenty minutes or so, and then he got in his car and drove off. The phone rang maybe five minutes later. He called and my mom answered the phone. She handed it to me and said, "It's him." He said, "I've got a gun, I'm going to kill you." And I said, "I'm not leaving." And so I stayed there, ready for whatever was going to happen that night, and he never came back. He didn't come back that night.

Zois: How were you prepared for it?

Charles: I was going to see where he came in and I was going to jump him.

Zois: In your mind what would you do to him? You

had the thought he'd come in with a gun to kill you.

Charles: I had a frying pan, and I was going to smack him in the head.

Zois: Uh-huh. And in your mind, what would happen if you hit him in the head with a frying pan?

Charles: That it would probably knock him out.

Zois: You say it would probably knock him out.

Charles: Yes.

Zois: How heavy was the frying pan?

Charles: It was pretty big.

Zois: It was a big frying pan.

Charles: A big cast-iron frying pan.

Zois: And how would you have struck him?

Charles: With everything I had.

Zois: With all of your force.

Charles: Yes.

Zois: Across the head.

Charles: Yes.

Zois: Where on the head?

Charles: I don't know; I wasn't thinking about that. Just that I would get the best shot I could. I knew that I probably had only one, so it should be a good one.

Zois: And in your mind what would happen to him when you hit him with the frying pan?

Charles: Then my thoughts were that the cops would come.

Zois: What would happen to him?

Charles: He'd be out cold.

Zois: How cold?

Charles: Not dead.

Zois: You had the thought, though, that it could kill him.

Charles: I had the thought that, yeah. I wasn't—That wasn't—I was just trying to defend myself, wasn't trying to kill him, just trying to get a good shot.

Zois: Right, but your thought was that when you hit him with the frying pan you could kill him.

Charles: I don't think that went through my mind.

Zois: You said yes a minute ago. Now you're waffling on it.

Charles: It's pretty hard for me to think of, killing somebody, so I think I may have known in my mind, but I tried to suppress it.

Zois: Have you had thoughts of killing him?

Charles: Not recently, but during those times I did, yes.

Zois: You did.

Charles: Yes.

Zois: So you had the thought of killing him? And then that night he calls and says he's got a gun, and so you armed yourself with a heavy frying pan, and your thought was that you would hit him as hard as you could across the head. And you had the thought that he could die.

Charles: Yes.

Zois: Now, if you look at that, did you want to kill him?

Charles: I think I probably would have.

Zois: You say, "I think."

Charles: It's a hard thing to come to grips with.

Zois: I understand that. I see how difficult it is for you to come to grips with your rage.

Charles: I'd thought about it before, so I presume yes.

Zois: "I presume." Did you want to kill him?

Charles: Yes, I guess I did. Yes, I did.

Zois: So you had these thoughts in your mind?

Charles: Yes.

At the beginning of the evaluation, Charles's face had been somewhat stoical and immobile. Now his eyes take on a sad aura. The muscles around his mouth relax; his lips are no longer pursed.

I am concentrating on two things. First, I continue to focus on and sift through Charles's defenses in an effort to get him to look at his underlying emotions. Second, I place great emphasis on detail as I ask him to describe the circumstances of that night. By constantly pushing for narrative rather than summary, I encourage Charles to put himself back in that moment, to reexperience it emotionally in the telling.

Summary is one way in which people attempt to avoid reliving painful episodes and the emotions connected with them; it makes intellectualization, rationalization, and other defenses much easier to employ. Attention to detail stimulates the person to relive the event.

Putting the Feelings in Balance

Short-term therapists strive to help patients perceive the balance of feelings that exist in almost all relationships. A discovery of positive feelings that previously were obscured by overwhelmingly negative ones can help release you from an anger or sense of hurt that has dominated your life; it can free you from a guilt that strangles your ability to live with satisfaction and a sense of harmony with your world.

This segment immediately followed the one above.

Zois: So you had these thoughts in your mind?

Charles: Yes.

Zois: How do you feel right now as you think about them?

Charles: (After a long pause) I hate once again that it seems so simple. It's just so simple and easy once again to draw up these horrible feelings, and I'd like to get rid of them. (Tearfully) I can't exorcise them. I can't. There's nothing I can do to get rid of them.

Zois: So you're in a lot of pain that you wanted to kill this man.

Charles: Yes.

Zois: You have very mixed feelings about him.

Charles: Yes, I felt for him also. He's a very pathetic character, too. It was never that clear. There was always that part of him... He was so horribly inconsistent. Sometimes the rage was all-consuming, and sometimes I would see him as such a pathetic person that... how could I have such rage against this guy who couldn't even... could just barely get through life by himself? Yet I resented the fact that I was put upon.

Charles sums up the emotional conflict within all of us that causes mixed feelings toward significant people in our lives. In most instances, we focus only on our anger or our sense of being cheated or victimized. We push aside the tender feelings that coexist with the stronger painful one. We place those tender feelings beyond recall.

I help Charles move from his static anger and sense of victimization to a more dynamic acknowledgment of the tender and guilty feelings he has about his stepfather. How could he be so enraged at this man when he also empathizes with him? Resentment at being put in such a dilemma is a universal issue, and admitting both sets of feelings serves to lessen the paralysis engendered when a strong emotion dominates our lives.

Zois: So you have very mixed feelings about him.

Charles: Yes, obviously.

Zois: On the one hand, he was the father you hoped for, and on the other he was this man who was lashing out at your mother and lashing out at you, and it was very painful for you to acknowledge.

Charles: I see him now, and part of the reason that that dinner I was telling you about and the other family situations are horrendous is because I have to pretend that nothing ever happened. You can't be honest with him. So I feign indifference.

Zois: So you have dealt with these very intense feelings by avoidance.

Charles: There have been times when I've been honest with them, and then they just shut me out. [This is the defense of *rationalization*. I don't point out that Charles is rationalizing, however, because I don't want to interrupt his progress in expressing his feelings about his stepfather.]

Zois: We're talking about your stepfather. Have you ever declared your feelings to him?

Charles: Yes.

Zois: What'd you say?

Charles: It's been a while, but I said that I couldn't stand what he did to me and that I resented the fact that I was in a situation where all I had to do was react. That I just reacted to his shit, that I felt I was never in control of what went on.

Zois: But did you ever declare to him how you felt about him?

Charles: Yes.

Zois: What did you say?

Charles: That I couldn't stand him.

Zois: Did you ever declare your positive feelings toward him? Did you ever declare the concern you had for him when you saw him as weak and crippled?

Charles: No. That's also hard. I could easily say why I was angry, that I hated him, but I never could tell him I saw that he had a soft side.

Zois: So it was easy to keep a distance from him by declaring your rage, but it was very difficult for you to be close to him by declaring your positive feelings.

Charles: Impossible.

Zois: How old is your stepfather?

Charles: Sixty something, sixty-five.

Zois: Have you had thoughts about the day when he would die?

Charles: Yes, I have.

Zois: What are your thoughts?

Charles: I thought it would be a release, that I probably would feel guilty because I had never really addressed it to him.

Zois: So where's the release?

Charles: That he'd be gone.

Zois: But you'd still be left with your guilt. So this is another situation that you're setting up that you'll be left in the middle of nowhere, that when that day comes to put him in his coffin and say your last good-bye, he'll be a voice from the grave for you, that you are not prepared to say good-bye, that you will not have resolved it if it goes on like this, and he'll be in his grave, and you'll be guilty. So there's this element here of self-punishment and self-defeat that's very strong.

I present this interpretation, which sums up the core conflicts of Charles's life, in very strong language. I hoped the image of putting his stepfather in a coffin would have a startling enough impact to stimulate the feelings he will be left with if he does not resolve the relationship. Once Charles acknowledges his emotions and experiences them with me, I take care to point out what the core conflict has accomplished and what the result will be if there is no change.

A pivotal point is reached when the therapist helps a person who has become an angry victim move away from that negative mode to an acknowledgment of his tender feelings; that acknowledgment is what allows for a balanced view of the relationship and for the development of intimacy. Charles's anger doesn't go away, but it becomes balanced with tenderness. Then the tender feelings and the balanced view work together to produce a successful resolution of his conflicted feelings.

Every relationship contains opposing emotions. Once you understand that, you open the door to intimacy, because you have banished the phantoms, the emotions and impulses that accompany a conflicted and unbalanced view of a relationship—guilt, chronic grief, rage, self-sabotage.

Moving toward Intimacy

Intimacy is letting other people see your most important thoughts and feelings, and sharing emotional experiences with them. It is allowing other people to be useful to you. Intimacy is therapeutic and curative.

Man may be a social animal, but he is not by nature an intimate animal. Intimacy is a skill that must be learned. Sadly, because intimacy is often fraught with anxiety and is associated with painful rather than positive experiences, as a protective mechanism many people avoid it.

The converse of intimacy is physical and emotional isolation—the absence of contact with the world around you. When you are isolated, information is transmitted with great difficulty between you and the surrounding world. Only with intimacy can you open yourself to the world. All kinds of benefits emanate from this emotional sharing and mutual usefulness.

Thus, in its broadest sense, intimacy allows you to live life. It encompasses everything from saying hello at the corner newsstand to dealing with co-workers, meeting friends for dinner, going home to the person or people who are important to you, telephoning your parents or your brother or sister. When you are isolated, none of those contacts can exist in a way that leads you to inner happiness.

If you don't allow the therapist to become intimate with you, the therapy's not going to go anywhere. The therapist won't be able to be truly useful to you. At many points along the way, you may struggle to keep the therapist at arm's length. But the persistence of the short-term therapist in breaking through your defenses allows your painful emotions and memories to come to the surface quickly. Then—and most important—the process allows you to share those emotions and that information with your therapist. When you share your feelings with the therapist, the two of you establish intimacy; you allow the therapist to be useful to you.

In short-term therapy, no question or dialogue is superfluous; everything is geared toward accomplishing an end. Thus far these segments of my initial session with Charles have been in sequence, but here is a segment from earlier in the session. We are discussing the fact that he had expected to see Dr. Frank at this session.

Here I utilize a discussion of Dr. Frank to explore the issue of intimacy and the problems he has experienced when he allowed himself to feel close to someone.

Zois: So you had thoughts that you would see her again.
Charles: Yes, I assumed I would see her again, and
             you probably next week.
Zois: So how did you feel that you didn't see her today?
Charles: I was a little surprised.
Zois: What was the feeling?
Charles: I felt that I was going to be sort of kept
             somehow off balance.
Zois: What's the feeling that goes along with the idea
             that she's going to keep you off balance?

Charles: Not her, it was just the change.

Zois: But how did you feel that you weren't going to see her?

Charles: A little disappointed.

Zois: So what was that feeling like? What did it feel like to be disappointed that she wasn't here today for you?

Charles: A sense of loss.

Zois: How does it feel that you lost her today?

Charles: It's a little upsetting.

Zois: You say "a little upsetting." You want to minimize it.

Charles: It's not a maximum situation. The purpose of my being here is not friendship; it's—

Zois: But the reality doesn't help the way you feel. You had feelings about her, and you had a sense of loss when you didn't see her here. How do you feel as you think about that?

Charles: I don't know. Sometimes... I don't want to intellectualize.

Zois: But you *are* intellectualizing.

Charles: I can't seem to put it in the same terms that you do.

Zois: But you intellectualize, and you tell me that you're helpless here to declare your feelings, just like about your brother. But we see your feelings about your brother are very clear. It's just your anxiety about declaring them. So you can be very specific when you want to be. And now with Dr. Frank and your positive feelings toward her, again you're having trouble declaring them. You're saying it was a sense of loss.

Charles: I was disappointed in not seeing her, but it doesn't mean I'm—

Zois: Now, you see, you're intellectualizing. What was the feeling at your sense of loss and disappointment?

Charles: I think you're magnifying it.

Zois: Now you're analyzing me. You're doing everything but answering the question about your feelings. So you see there's a part of you that wants to keep a distance from me. You don't want to tell me your intimate thoughts and feelings. If I don't stay right on top of it with you and ask you to look at it, then you will take a passive position and stay behind a wall that you're building here between the two of us. So again the issue is, what's going to happen if you keep that wall up?

Charles: It means that I'm not going to grow, I'm not going to change, I'm going to be mired in the same damn situation, which I don't want.

Zois: So there's a part of you that wants change, and there's another part of you that wants to make me useless. You look sad right now.

Charles: Yes, I am. It's the realization of that. It's not that I haven't known it before, it's just that...

Zois: You look tearful to me. Are you?

Charles: Yes, because—

Zois: Are you holding those tears back?

Charles: No, no, it's...

Zois: But you look sad that you make me useless to you.

Charles: It's the realization of what I know, what I know... that there's two parts of myself.

Zois: But they're in operation here, and there's a part of you that doesn't want me to penetrate into your life, doesn't want me to be close to you, share your intimate thoughts and feelings. So that, when it comes time here to say good-bye to one another, I'll be a useless man. You'll leave here with your own feelings within you, not having shown them to me.

Charles: Yes, and I don't want that.

At the end of the evaluation session, I again bring up the issue of intimacy.

Zois: So we've talked here and touched on some of these issues in a surface way. Now at this time do you believe this therapy can be of help to you, discussing these issues? Is this something you want to go through?

Charles: Yes.

Zois: How do you feel about our meeting here today?

Charles: I feel positive about it.

Zois: In what sense?

Charles: That it's difficult.... It is... It forces me to focus on the things in my life that aren't working, that I want to change. That it's not easy, but I want to work at it. I don't know if it can come to anything, necessarily, but it's a step.

Zois: You see, you say you don't know if it can come to anything.

Charles: I want it to come to something.

Zois: Well, which is it? Again, you want to do what you've done to everybody else in your life: leave the situation. You reach out and then you pull back and you get behind your wall. So on the one hand here you tell me that you want to change your life and you believe this is going to be helpful, and then you go to "I don't know if it's going to come to anything." So you're the master of your fate here, and if you want to make this situation useless to you, you're perfectly capable of doing that. I mean, your problems are your problems. I can fail here. You stay behind your wall and I'll be defeated. But I can afford to fail.

The patient frequently views the therapist as omnipotent. Such a perspective increases the patient's tendency to be passive and to allow the therapist to do the work. My statement that I can fail also underscores the need for Charles to take responsibility for his role in succeeding or failing.

Charles: But I can't.
Zois: Well, that's the issue. But do you see what you do here with me now, in this moment, what you do with everybody in your life, that you put your toe in the water and then you back off and you don't jump in?
Charles: Yes.
Zois: This is a very important issue for you to look at, that if in our work here you persist like this, then I'll be useless to you and you'll say good-bye to me at the end of whatever time, and I'll take my place next to your mother, your brother, your stepfather, and any other number of people. Do you see that?

Between the beginning and the end of this evaluation session, Charles achieved closeness with me and I with him. Although he is a highly resistant person, in less than ninety minutes he has gotten in touch with some of the worst things he believes about himself; he has shown me emotions that he had bottled up and not shown anyone before. That accomplishment is essential to his bringing about change in his life.

Even though the evaluation has been a success, my final statement to Charles is not congratulatory. I put him on notice that what we have done is just the beginning of a journey that will have many twists and turns. I leave him with this thought: he's got to work on this.

Charles completed his journey. Five years after treatment, on routine follow-up, he reports that he lives a life of greater satisfaction, in which his relationships are more positive than in the past. He says that his view of himself has changed dramatically for the better.

Completing the Treatment

Your therapist is obligated to do a careful scrutiny of the issues that confront you when you come in for your first session. As the therapy progresses, your therapist must assess how you are dealing with those issues, how you feel, and how you are functioning in the problematic areas of your life.

In determining when the therapy is complete, you are the only barometer. You enter therapy with certain issues, as well as a greater or lesser degree of resistance to looking at them. Your therapy is complete when you report that you feel better and when you can objectively state that you are dealing with the most difficult issues in your life—and with other issues as well—in a way that you perceive to be more effective and productive.

The evidence that you are dealing with your problems more successfully is that you are experiencing your life in a more satisfying way. You are not running from the conflicts that burdened you when you first came in, nor are you troubled with unexamined pain, sadness, anger, depression, or guilt. At the end of therapy you can look back on those emotions and on the early sessions and say, in effect, "It's difficult to believe that I was so confused and bewildered, that I was dealing with the world around me in this way." Then and only then is the therapy complete.

You are feeling better and doing better, but will this improved situation last? That, in the end, is the important question. In my practice I conduct videotaped follow-up sessions with patients—ideally after one, three, and five years—in which I reassess the issues that originally brought them into treatment. I also examine the problems that exist in their current lives. It's a way—really the only way—I can affirm that the therapy was effective.

For anyone at any remove from therapy, continued awareness and vigilance are essential. Staying well balanced emotionally requires at least as much effort as keeping fit physically.

CHAPTER 2

Short-Term Therapy: Why It's Better

Short-term therapy is a no-nonsense technique for rapidly and effectively tackling the emotional problems that beset most of us. In traditional, long-term psychotherapies these problems have been addressed by nonproductive approaches that are ambiguous, unpredictable, and needlessly time-consuming.

The short-term therapy I practice is in-depth psychotherapy based on the ideas of Freud, Alexander, Davanloo, Malan, Mann, Reich, and Sifneos (see the Bibliography). The focus is on the patient's past experiences, current life, fantasies, and dreams. Short-term therapy works on the deepest levels of the unconscious.

The short-term technique actively cuts through the defenses—the vagueness, rationalizations, intellectualizations, and other smoke screens we create in order to hide the truth from ourselves. When your defenses are eliminated, you break through to the underlying issues that give rise to your unhappiness. In a clear and focused process of examining and confronting these issues, you come to a resolution of your problems.

How short is short-term therapy? It varies. If, as with most patients, the therapy takes place once a week, it can require from several weeks to as many as eight or ten months.

Short-term therapy accomplishes everything that long-term therapy can accomplish, but does it faster and better. How can a complete and thorough therapy take place in such a short period of time when most analytically based therapies take two to five years or longer? The answer is simple: through active probing.

The refinement of a technique often lags behind the development of a scientific theory. No one criticizes Copernicus for not substantiating his theories; he did not have the technology to do so. Likewise, Freud brilliantly conceptualized the structure of the psyche and knew what had to be accomplished in a therapy. But it is unfair to expect that, with the relatively meager accumulation of data available to him, Freud should have been able to develop an effective technique for treating people.

Psychoanalysis and related therapies have always been top-heavy with theories, many of which have taken on an aura of absolutism, becoming static and stagnant in the process. In the absence of a technique, traditional therapists continue to argue about theory in much the way theologians dispute religious issues. Until the last decade or so, therapists learned theories and then groped for ways of working that would validate them. That approach had enormous implications for the methods of treatment that evolved, because often they were tailored to suit preconceived ideas.

Short-term therapists reverse that approach. Using videotaped documentation, we have been able to develop a technique based on a step-by-step analysis of therapy sessions. Some results validate existing theories; other results contradict them. We base our evolving theories on our empirical observations of the videotaped record, incorporating our findings into existing theory or modifying that theory according to what has actually happened in therapy sessions.

The Key Role of Videotaping

Scientific theory continuously evolves; it's a dynamic, existential process. The only way to bring about change in psychotherapeutic concepts and attitudes is to have a technique that is demonstrable, that can be studied.

Videotape technology has allowed the development of such a technique. Therapists can now create a record of the application of a technique and the patient's response. Instead of relying on esoteric theories to explain behavior, the short-term therapist observes the results of therapeutic interactions and crafts a technique based on those observations. The video camera has done for psychotherapy what the electron microscope has done for biology. It has brought therapy into the modern world. Moreover, videotaping allows accountability in what has been a very inexact science.

I want to stress that I am speaking only of the need for *therapists* to share the data recorded in sessions. In no way do I advocate the dissemination of information about patients in any other quarter. Patients who allow their sessions to be videotaped are aware that the tapes will be used for training and research purposes.

Before videotape technology was available, it was difficult to create useful records of therapy sessions. Handwritten notes are subjective and depend on how much the therapist can remember, and audio recording is not a good substitute for the audiovisual image of patient and therapist.

Videotaping allows for careful scrutiny of the therapeutic process. When not only the spoken word but the mannerisms and the facial expressions of both patient and therapist can be documented, an exhaustive microanalysis can be done of the interaction and a wealth of information can be gleaned. Therapists can study in detail how they and other therapists have conducted sessions, and the technique can continuously evolve. Videotaping sessions makes the short-term technique a uniquely demonstrable one that validates or invalidates any theory and allows theory to be refined.

The material that the patient provides sometimes validates hypotheses and sometimes stimulates modification of what formerly was sacrosanct psychoanalytic theory. For example, Freud emphasized sexuality and aggressive impulses as the key elements in what he referred to as the unconscious. When we study videotapes of patients' responses to focused questioning, we see that they struggle with other feelings as well—pain, grief, hurt, sadness, guilt—and that these issues are as important as aggression and sexuality, if not more so. Most of the information presented in this book is derived from insights gained during more than a decade of studying the videotaped therapy sessions of hundreds of patients.

Some critics maintain that videotaping therapy sessions and sharing that information with other mental health professionals violates the confidentiality that long-term therapists traditionally have maintained. But where did the notion of confidentiality come from in the first place? It originally arose as an apology, a rationalization by early analysts and therapists who did not have the means to document, shape, and refine a technique. If videotape technology had existed in the early days of psychoanalysis, confidentiality would not have emerged as a credo.

With the advent of videotape technology, the questionable concept of confidentiality—which, far from having a positive value, can reinforce a patient's sense of shame and guilt—must fade into the past, and therapists must come to see the value of documenting their work and sharing and explicating it with their colleagues. Doing this means that members of the therapeutic community must achieve some degree of intimacy among themselves.

If you don't have a demonstrable technique, you don't have an effective therapy. In my discussions with critics of short-term therapy, my attitude is: show me yours and I'll show you mine. On what documented body of knowledge do other therapists base their statements and assumptions? Unlike therapists who don't videotape, short-term therapists have reference to a body of information that is available for scrutiny.

A colleague can ask me, "How do you deal with a case of pathological mourning?" and I can offer five or six tapes. "How do you deal with a patient who becomes angry at you?" Several tapes will demonstrate. It is through constant reference to videotaped sessions that the short-term technique has evolved and short-term therapists have learned their profession.

Therapists are not artists. The artist can intuit what the therapist cannot. Therapists must systematically observe and refine their information, and that can't be done by referring to notes made after the session. Reports from therapists who don't videotape are similar to what Plato spoke of in his allegory of the cave: shadows on the wall.

Myths Exploded by Short-Term Therapy

Certain self-perpetuating beliefs have helped define the accepted process of therapy. The problem is that these ideas don't hold up, particularly in the face of the documented short-term technique.

Myth: Long-Term Problems Require Long-Term Solutions

If the therapist believes a long-term problem needs a

long-term solution, then the treatment is going to take a long time.

Many therapists and patients fall prey to self-fulfilling prophecies. Volumes have been written about how children learn slowly if a teacher's expectation of them is low. If the expectation of therapists is that patients are slow learners— and, for therapy to take several years, that has to be the assumption—those therapists have little respect for the intelligence of their patients. Furthermore, the therapists' mind-set will prevail.

Long-term, open-ended therapies generally fail at the outset to clarify what exactly is wrong with the patient. This failure, this vagueness, has caused the traditional therapeutic community to come up with such rationalizations as "It takes a long time to get to know the patient" and "Long-term problems need long-term solutions." The reply of the short-term therapist is "Not if the therapist knows how to apply an effective technique."

After the initial clarification of the patient's problems, short-term therapy expedites the process of emotional change. Rather than allowing the patient to be resistant, the therapist declares war on the patient's defenses and breaks through them. Then, along with the patient, the therapist uncovers the "loaded" emotional material that is at the core of the patient's problems.

Traditional long-term therapy that is open-ended and ambiguous is unpredictable. Because the therapist does not develop a strategy that includes an estimate of how long the therapy will take, progress is difficult to perceive and assess. In contrast, because it's built on a specific technique and designed to be effective within a brief period of time, short-term therapy lends itself to objective evaluation. It is predictable.

There's also a benefit for the therapist in shortening the length of treatment: the short-term approach allows therapists to work with many more patients, which enhances their effectiveness with each individual. If the process took twenty years, I might just now be finishing the first cases I took on after my residency. But with short-term therapy in those twenty years I have repeated the process many times and accumulated a considerable body of knowledge and experience that I can evaluate and put to use.

Myth: Patients Can Resolve Their Problems through Free Association

Some aspects of therapy have changed since Freud's time. Most people can't afford to attend sessions four or five times a week, as was once the norm. Therapy is now more commonly scheduled once or twice a week, and most patients sit facing the therapist rather than reclining on a couch. But free association and a passive approach on the part of the therapist continue to be hallmarks of many therapies.

When Freud first started his work, the first thing he encountered was the patient's resistance, which he called the defenses. In order to overcome resistance, Freud tried making suggestions—"This is what you should do"—but that didn't work. He tried hypnosis and again was unsuccessful. He then turned to the technique of free association.

The theory is simple: if the therapist takes a passive, nondirective stance and allows patients to talk freely, the repressed material that they are defending against will eventually work its way to the surface. In other words, the patients themselves will come to various realizations, with very limited intervention from the therapist, and that activity will have a therapeutic, curative effect.

But is this so? If you freely associate, does the painful material in fact work its way to the surface? Does it happen in the majority of people or does it happen rarely? The process of free association itself—its duration and the lack of documentation—makes its efficacy impossible to validate.

Only one thing is certain: if patients are encouraged merely to free-associate and are permitted to use defenses without intervention by the therapist, the therapeutic process will take a long time and the results will be questionable.

Traditional treatment by a passive therapist is unnecessarily long, prolonging the patient's suffering as well as increasing the cost. Moreover, in a long-term process there is a chronic risk that the patient will intellectualize, rationalize, and use other defenses rather than talk about issues in a productive way.

Short-term therapists operate on the belief that, because the core emotions are painful, patients who are allowed to freely associate—to be vague, to rationalize, and to repeat themselves—will in most cases stay away from the very issues they need to confront. We therefore take an active role in getting the patient past the defenses to a confrontation with those issues.

Myth: You Should Discuss Certain Matters Only with Your Therapist

Earlier I spoke about confidentiality as an issue that arises among therapists, who debate whether they should view one another's videotaped sessions for the purposes of research and teaching. The concept of confidentiality can also affect the therapy from the patient's point of view, for it implies that people have unique thoughts and feelings that should not be aired outside therapy.

A person may have thoughts on any subject: a wish that a parent would die, sexual fantasies, homicidal impulses. Sometimes we consider ourselves freaks, sadistic maniacs, even potential murderers because of these thoughts. On a less dramatic level, we are often reluctant to talk to others about feelings of inadequacy, anger, or guilt; we may even have trouble admitting such feelings to ourselves.

Because the confidentiality that is part of traditional

therapies can encourage patients to believe that the feelings discussed in therapy are shameful, the videotaping that is done for purposes of documentation functions as a therapeutic tool as well. It cuts against the grain of the patient's neurotic guilt, the notion that the matters discussed in therapy are terrible and should be hidden from others. It is essential to break through this notion, for it inhibits the important ability to be intimate with others.

Toward the end of their therapies, many of my patients have viewed with me segments of tapes of their evaluation and early sessions, and have expressed how valuable it was to see themselves as they were at that time.

In 400 B.C., the typical Athenian didn't really believe in all the Greek deities. Yet when Socrates was put on trial, one of the charges against him was religious heresy.

It's the same with traditional therapy today. Many jokes and comedy routines center around the myths of long-term treatment. Yet these notions are strenuously upheld by the therapeutic community, which is wary of the short-term therapists' ability to accomplish in a brief period of time what it takes other practitioners years to accomplish, if in fact they accomplish anything at all.

Questions and Answers about Short-Term Therapy

Is Short-Term Therapy Just a Quick Fix?

Although it is useful in crisis work, short-term therapy is not crisis intervention, which has a more limited scope in that it is aimed at a patient's specific, current problem. Nor are we talking about supportive therapy or directive therapy, neither of which takes an analytic approach that connects the emotions of the past with those of the present. In those modes, therapists recognize the patients' self-destructive behavior and provide them with a reflection of what they're doing, along with advice.

Short-term therapy, like traditional analytical therapy, focuses on emotions, thoughts, and experiences that have been buried. The short-term therapist actively challenges the patient's defenses to gain access to his deep emotions. It is actually more systematic than long-term therapy in probing the major issues of the patient's life, past and present.

Will the change that takes place be permanent? Videotapes of follow-up sessions conducted one, three, and five years after the end of treatment demonstrate the efficacy of the short-term technique. However, emotional health is an evolutionary process. The results of the curative process will be as permanent as anything else that we do—if we work at it. If we don't remain vigilant of our emotions, attitudes, and behavior, the gains made in therapy will be as permanent as physical fitness when diet and exercise are not maintained.

Is Short-Term Therapy Geared to Giving Advice?

Not at all. Advice is something that you can get from anybody but you shouldn't look for it from a therapist, whose ability to give it is indeterminable. A therapist's advice may be as good as or worse than what your best friend tells you.

The giving of advice provides no lasting therapeutic effect, nor do supportive statements—"I'm sure your mother loved you" or "You really weren't cruel to your brother" —or siding with a patient about what her husband or co-worker has done. Yet if the therapist does not understand the dynamics of conducting a therapy or is not having a therapeutic impact, the impulse to give advice or to commiserate with the patient can be strong.

Productive activity on the part of the therapist challenges the defenses and enables the patient to get to underlying thoughts, memories, and emotions. The goal of that activity is to produce self-awareness and emotional change.

Does Short-Term Therapy Put a Lot of Pressure on the Patient?

The short-term therapist puts pressure on patients to commit themselves, to be clear, and, in a joint endeavor with the therapist, to take action and face the most painful, disconcerting, upsetting, and guilt-provoking issues in their lives. In that sense there is pressure. But this is pressure that most people can deal with.

You will always feel some degree of discomfort and pain when you face what you consider to be the worst things about yourself, things you didn't think you wanted to reveal even to yourself. However, there is no growth without this kind of acknowledgment. If you really want to change, you have to face your shortcomings. You have to take that step, run that risk, and tolerate the anxiety that goes along with accomplishing change.

Short-term therapists are sometimes accused of badgering patients, of pressuring them to give a "correct" response. The best reply to this charge is an invitation to review videotapes and analyze, in detail and in context, the exchange between therapist and patient. The verbatim record of the conversation between Charles and me demonstrates that I did not put words in his mouth. Every statement I examined with him was his. I scrutinized *his* words and asked him to elaborate on *his* concepts.

As a related point, compliance—agreeing with the therapist's interpretations and statements—is so commonplace in all types of therapy that the therapist must be vigilant and challenge it whenever it occurs. Compliance serves as a defense, as one way for the patient to avoid digesting the information that the therapy generates. By complying, a patient can avoid experiencing the emotional component of the material. In *Character Analysis* (1933), a book that enumerates many concepts that underlie much short-term therapy technique, Wilhelm Reich describes the compliant, or polite, patient as exercising a resistance—that is, using compliance to cover up underlying aggressive impulses.

At one point during the evaluation session, I wanted to assure myself that Charles was not being compliant; he may have been agreeing with me but not really experiencing an emotional component of the recognition.

Zois: Again, you retreat to a helpless position. We see there's a part of you that wants to keep this whole thing in limbo. That these people will be strangers to you, they'll die, and you'll carry the guilt around for the rest of your life and perpetuate defeating yourself, not allowing yourself to have anything more than the minimum. Hmm?

Charles: Yes.

Zois: Do you see that or are you just agreeing with me?

Charles: Yeah, I see it.

Zois: How do you feel right now here with me?

Charles: Just sad because I didn't deal with it before.

If I had determined that Charles was being compliant, I would have dealt with his response as with any other defense, beginning by bringing it to his attention.

Traditional therapists might claim that short-term therapy, by putting pressure on the defenses, will make the patient worse. But videotaping proves that we don't make people worse. We make them better, and more quickly. Our patients immediately understand that we are working in their best interest, that they may be in unfamiliar waters but that's where they should be, despite their defenses. Some therapists tend to be afraid they are going to lose patients if they upset them, but in truth the reverse happens. The patient forms a strong connection with a therapist who is active. Covertly or overtly, the patient acknowledges, "This person is willing to go down the road with me."

Does Transference Take Place in Short-Term Therapy?

Patients come into therapy with strong feelings about the important people in their lives; they tend to transfer those feelings to the therapist. Therapists use this *neurotic transference* to help patients work through their conflicts. This process takes place in short-term therapy as well as in long-term treatment.

Traditional therapists ask how people in short-term therapy—ten, twenty, or thirty sessions—are able to say good-bye to the therapist in an appropriate way. They are concerned that in such a brief therapy there isn't enough time to work through the neurotic transference, that patients will have incorporated the therapist into their psychic universe and won't be able to say good-bye easily, won't be able to withstand the loss of the therapist.

The short-term technique includes constant scrutiny and interpretation of the patient's emotions toward the therapist, not only of emotions that stem from the transference but also of the patient's genuine feelings toward the therapist, which in traditional therapy are not often talked about. These genuine feelings—often positive—are not part of the transference but are the patient's responses to someone who attempts to help him with his life. Through constant examination of both the neurotic transference and the genuine positive feelings, therapist and patient achieve the intimacy that facilitates the resolution of emotional pain.

"How do you feel with me here today?"
"You know, you keep asking me that. You asked me that the last time."

"How do you feel with me here today?"

"I had a dream about you. You went along on a fishing trip with my dad and me."

"How do you feel with me here today?"
"You annoyed me by being five minutes late."

Keeping at it all the time prevents the patient from working repressed, unconscious, or neurotic material into an attachment with the therapist that can't be forgone. It keeps the therapist very clearly in focus for the patient. Constantly clearing the air of positive and negative feelings toward the therapist can go a long way toward aborting the neurotic transference and allowing a smooth completion of treatment.

When I judge that the therapy is approaching the termination phase, I ask this question: "Have you thought about the day when we will say good-bye to each other?" Sometimes my patients don't want to deal with that question; instead of expressing their feelings, they say to me, "Well, I know I can always call you up and see you again." These patients want to avoid the good-bye. Then I say, "What if you got a phone call tomorrow telling you I had died?" I force my patients to confront the idea of the final good-bye with me, and I use elements of the short-term technique to explore the unresolved deep feelings that make the good-bye difficult. I don't leave that door open.

Keeping a patient in therapy interminably fosters the neurotic transference. The therapist becomes a part of the patient's life.

The ability to deal with loss is one of the major issues in all of our lives, and, just as they haven't wanted to give up other attachments to significant figures, patients often don't want therapy to end. However, if the therapist has applied the short-term technique effectively—has consistently challenged and focused on the patient's resistance; has examined the patient's emotions with significant people; has dealt with the issue of intimacy and usefulness between patient and therapist; and has consistently scrutinized both the transference and the patient's genuine feelings toward the therapist—then saying good-bye need not be a stumbling block to completing treatment.

Are There Dangers in Suddenly Facing a Strong Underlying Emotion?

There are no dangers for functional people, those who fall into the category psychiatrists call neurotic. These people may be in pain, but they have some sense of themselves and their activities in relation to other people and the world around them. Although they suffer from emotional maladies based on past and current experiences, and although they may engage in self-defeating behavior, they are able to function reasonably well; for example, they have a job or career, and they interact with other people and family members.

Years ago, traditional therapists considered breaking through the defenses a dangerous process, but it now has been well documented that functional people not only can tolerate these emotions but can work with them and improve their ability to handle them.

Is Short-Term Therapy for Everyone?

Short-term therapy is not for people who have had a divorce from reality, who are unable to function because their view of the world has been distorted by severe mental illness. It is not for psychotic people who have had to use medications or have been institutionalized for treatment.

Short-term therapy is for people who can stand to view things about themselves that they ordinarily might not acknowledge, even to themselves. Patients must be able to tolerate painful material from the past that they tend to diminish or ignore.

Most people are candidates for short-term therapy, as long as they are neurotic as opposed to psychotic. Short-term therapy is geared for that large segment of the population that, although functional, could conduct their personal, social, and professional lives with more satisfaction and happiness.

CHAPTER 3

Masks, Shields, and Cover-ups

Your best friend remarks that you've put on some weight. Your reaction is:

a. To admit you've gained two or three pounds when you know it's more like ten.
b. To accuse your friend of attacking you.
c. To stay home that night instead of going to a party.
d. To realize that it's time to start cutting back on the pizza and ice cream.

At the family Thanksgiving dinner, you sense that you and your brother are moving toward an argument. Your reaction is:

a. To change the subject.
b. To profess ignorance and let him win.
c. To try as hard as you can to make your point crystal

clear, meanwhile thinking how stubborn he has always been.

d. To listen to what he says and then explain your thoughts and feelings.

You are passed over for a raise and a promotion at work. Your reaction is:

a. To say, "How important is financial success anyway?"
b. To think, I never liked the boss anyway. Now I know he's a real idiot. He is not capable of appreciating my talent. It doesn't bother me.
c. To begin focusing mainly on your own projects, paying little attention to the people around you.
d. To speak with your boss about your work and how you could improve it.

Your sister hurts your feelings by criticizing the way you dress. Your reaction is:

a. To ignore her comments.
b. To think, She's just jealous of my creative taste in clothes.
c. To answer her with, "So what? Your cooking stinks."
d. To let her know that her comments are hurtful to you.

In each situation, reactions *a*, *b*, and *c* involve a defense. Unless you chose reaction *d* all four times, you are capable of being defensive rather than meeting a difficult situation directly. If you chose *a*, *b*, or *c* once or more, you can count yourself a normal member of the human race, for we all use defenses.

What Are the Defenses and How Do They Work?

When the events and conflicts in our lives cause us emotional pain, we frequently adopt attitudes and ways of behaving that protect us from distress. Therapists call these attitudes and types of behavior defenses. Charles, whose evaluation session I presented in Chapter 1, was very defensive when he first entered therapy.

The defenses act as censors of that part of the psyche where your most painful feelings, memories, and impulses reside. You use the defenses in an attempt to cover up the private and subjective feelings that you would find unacceptable if you acknowledged them. Although the defenses mask your deepest emotions, those feelings cannot be quieted altogether; they insist on being heard anyway.

You are defensive in response to a sense of anger, hurt, or guilt about present or past events. Instead of telling yourself to look at the pain of a situation and to admit your own worst thoughts about what happened, you bury your unpleasant memories and try to avoid experiencing the emotions they generate. Because defenses keep you from facing important deep feelings, they frequently act as stumbling blocks to clear thinking and a sense of harmony with your world. When you create defenses against your anger, hurt, or guilt, you often punish yourself in the process. When your defenses become too intense, they prevent you from leading a full and satisfying life.

If it's not really possible and if it's self-defeating to do so, why do you try to silence your deep painful memories and feelings? You want to bury painful memories and their attendant emotions because they generate impulses that are anxiety-provoking or frightening.

An impulse is the response that an emotion generates. If the emotion is negative, the impulse generated is threatening. For example, when the emotion is rage, the impulse might be to lash out in a destructive way. When you sense such an impulse, you are disturbed because, *even though it's only a fantasy*, you perceive it as negative and unacceptable.

The impulses you're blocking when you use defenses generally exist within the realm of your fantasies. What you're resisting is your fear that an imagined worst-case scenario will come true. You deal with this fantasized impulse as though it is a real-life action that is going to erupt from within you, with dire consequences. In response, you marshal defenses that can be difficult to overcome. The more highly charged your memory of an event and the more intense your resulting negative emotion (guilt, rage, grief, or another strong feeling), the more intense will be the impulse generated by your emotion and the greater the array of defenses you erect to hide your distressing memories and feelings.

People who have many upsetting memories and highly charged emotions, and who consequently feel the threat of very intense impulses, often mount extraordinary defenses; they may even disassociate their thoughts from their emotions. Charles's memory of his impulse to kill his stepfather caused him great anxiety. In order to quiet that anxiety, he resisted attempts to get through to his underlying memories and emotions. Whenever a situation made him angry, he would become paralyzed in order to block the related impulse to lash out. Charles reacted to anger as though his fantasized desire to kill his stepfather had really happened and could happen again. He used a large number of defenses—principally passivity and avoidance—to block his anger. Finally, Charles responded to the memory of that night with guilt, which resulted in self-defeating, self-sabotaging behavior.

To summarize: An unpleasant event occurs. An emotion is attached to that event, and the emotion generates an impulse in you. All three—the event, the emotion, and the impulse—are charged with a great deal of distress and pain. You create defenses not only against the memory and the emotion attached to the memory but also, very importantly, against the impulse. That impulse gives rise to a notion that the fantasized action—for example, the desire to lash out in a violent way—has a reality to it. The impulse gives rise to anxiety, and you use your defenses to try to quell your anxiety.

Working Through Our Negative Emotions

What happens when your defenses are removed? What is the therapeutic process of working through your negative emotions so that they will become more manageable? An intellectual comprehension of your problems is not enough if you want to change and grow emotionally. Bringing a troubling emotion into the present is essential to the process of emotional change.

A therapist would begin by desensitizing you to your upsetting emotions and impulses. He or she would do this by asking specific questions and eliciting detailed responses concerning an event that stimulated the emotion.

When you recall a memory in detail, you relive the event and reexperience in the present the emotion attached to it. Only through detailed memories can you reexperience an emotion in its totality; if you describe a memory by means of a summary rather than a detailed narrative, the emotions generated by the memory are dissipated and minimized.

Desensitization is a gradual reduction of your anxiety about your emotions and the impulses associated with them. In desensitizing a person to an emotion, I focus on people and situations that are less intense before working toward those that are more highly charged. For example, I started with Charles's memory of anger toward his brother, which was not as deep and anxiety-ridden as the anger he felt toward his stepfather. If I had tried sooner to bring him to discuss a more significant experience of anger, his resistance would have been so great that the therapy would have become mired down or protracted, or might even have failed.

Describing the details of the fight with his stepfather allowed Charles to bring the emotions of that evening into the present and reexperience them with me. He relived what he had felt—all his terrible feelings of rage, guilt, and sorrow. When he relived his emotions in the present, Charles realized that rage had not been his only feeling. Other emotions had also been present, and he was able to take an inventory of them. He felt resentment because he was forced to take part in that kind of relationship, and he also felt sorrow and sympathy for his stepfather. He felt guilt and a great deal of self-hate because of the way he had dealt with his stepfather. His discovery of the other emotions that were attached to the event were important in helping Charles put his rage in perspective.

Charles's case illustrates how emotions give rise to anxiety and defenses: He remembered an event that generated an overwhelming emotion, which he viewed as his only response to that situation. That emotion generated an impulse to lash out, and the impulse produced anxiety, which clouded his ability to perceive the event clearly and objectively. His defenses arose in an effort to quell his anxiety, further obscuring his perceptions and his feelings.

Although we don't realize it, this type of anxiety exists in all of us. If something unpleasant occurs, we say, "It left a bad taste in my mouth," a metaphorical reference to the anxiety that accompanies a negative impulse. Anxiety complicates our ability to perceive clearly the issues in our lives.

Working through an emotion involves modifying it and attenuating the impulse it generates. The key to the process is taking inventory of the other emotions that were present. To do this, you examine a memory in detail and confront the overriding emotion that was generated, but you also bring to the surface the other emotions that were present but never acknowledged. As part of this process, you experience the impulse, but, because you now experience *all* of the emotions, the anxiety around the impulse is defused and you learn to tolerate it.

As the curtain of anxiety is drawn back and you see the emotion more objectively, it loses its darker component, and the impulse connected with it becomes comprehensible. As you acknowledge the other emotions, they give rise to a modified impulse that is not simply one-dimensional; it does not derive from only one aspect of the memory or from one intense emotion. The attenuated impulse is more complex because it is now connected to other emotions.

No relationship has one pure feeling and no others. When he reexperienced his hatred, Charles for the first time experienced all the other emotions and impulses that went along with it. He could say, in effect, "Wait a minute. There was a lot more to my feelings than just pure rage. There was sympathy for my stepfather. There was sorrow for him and for myself. There was guilt about what I thought I was going to do, and this guilt has paralyzed me." The hatred he felt was no longer all-pervasive. It was now mitigated, balanced, by his recognition of the other emotions that coexisted with it.

This process is very different from simply understanding that you have a problem with anger: it's not a matter of simply changing your mind about what happened. The therapist should not make supportive statements. When Charles stated that he wanted to kill his stepfather, I didn't try to change his mind, to make him believe that it really wasn't that way, because indeed it was that way. My goal was to get him to acknowledge for the first time all of the other emotional elements of that confrontation with his stepfather. That acknowledgment helped him work with the feelings that had been giving him trouble, tolerate the anxiety connected with his impulses, and come to a clearer perception of the totality of the experience, without denying the elements that he remembered and reacted to.

As you work through a painful emotion, you come to understand the enormous impact your unacknowledged feelings, impulses, and defenses have had within your private emotional world, in your relationships, in your work, and in your everyday life. As you see that you have engaged in negative and self-sabotaging behavior, sadness and depressive feelings arise. Dealing with these feelings is also part of the working-through process. With the realization that so much energy has gone in nonproductive directions, there also comes an awareness that you have the opportunity to make a choice.

At this point, you need to take action. You must answer a key question: What are you going to do about it? What action are you going to take based on the discovery you've made? You are at a crossroads. Will you take the victim role and say, "Poor me. Look what I did with my life," or will you use your new emotional perspective to gain strength? Will you draw on your resources and chart a new course?

A call to action is intrinsic to the short-term technique. When the therapist first poses the question "What are you going to do about remedying the problem?" many people respond with irritation, if not outright anger, because they are not accustomed to thinking in such terms about emotional issues. However, you are the only one who can translate your new self-awareness into changes in your behavior and attitudes.

The process of emotional change is not simple. A light bulb does not go on above your head as you arrive at a brilliant interpretation of your behavior. You do not suddenly shout "Eureka!" and run off—"cured"—into the sunset. Instead, a complex chain of events takes place. You learn to tolerate the anxiety of looking at an emotion that you have buried. The anxiety dissipates as the emotion and its attendant impulses take on a less formidable and threatening aspect. You begin to act on the knowledge that you now have an opportunity to approach life in a new way.

Because it is the first step in the process of emotional change, breaking through the defenses is a central element in the technique of short-term therapy. The therapist works in an active manner to make patients aware of their defenses. Only in this way can they explore the deeper issues that are causing pain and unhappiness.

Reading this book likewise will increase your awareness of your defenses. The discussions and self-explorations will help you see how you may be covering over deeper issues that result in self-defeating behavior. Chapters 6, 7, and 8 take up the topic of the defenses again, with a more comprehensive look at how they operate in three key areas of life: relationships, work, and your response to a loss. In the self-exploration of your own defenses at the end of Chapter 8, you are guided through a process of thought and feeling similar to that experienced in short-term therapy.

The Three Types of Defenses

People don't utilize just one defense. Typically we use several, sometimes alternately and sometimes in conjunction with one another.

The defenses fall into three categories. While we tend to favor one category over another, attitudes and behavior from all three often interact in our personalities.

The Defenses of Helplessness

Vagueness, relying on nonspecific thoughts and feelings, passivity, and adopting a victim role—these are all attempts to escape the pain of an event, an unpleasant memory, or an impulse to act in a negative way.

Vagueness. We commonly use vagueness to avoid making a commitment to a specific thought or feeling. People who use vagueness qualify important statements with such phrases as "I think," "I guess," "probably," "maybe," "I'm not sure," and "sometimes." Because they keep us from being focused and specific, generalizations such as "everybody" and "all the time" also function as a type of vagueness.

Such people tend to be ambivalent when it comes to important issues in their lives. Being vague and nonspecific inhibits clarity of thought and keeps you from focusing on what's really bothering you.

In my first session with Charles, he was vague in his responses when we talked about Dr. Frank, for example:

Zois: So it was Dr. Frank you were defensive against. Now here, with me, do you feel that way?
Charles: No, not particularly.
Zois: You say, "Not particularly"—you do or you don't.
Charles: I'm ambivalent.
Zois: You're sitting on the fence.
Charles: That's what I just said.
Zois: But what about that? You're having some difficulty taking a position with me.
Charles: Not with you per se.
Zois: But who else is here?

At a much more crucial point in the session, Charles again tried to retreat behind vague responses:

Zois: Now, if you look at that, did you want to kill him?
Charles: I think I probably would have...
Zois: You say, "I think."
Charles: It's a hard thing to come to grips with.
Zois: I understand that. I see how difficult it is for you to come to grips with your rage.
Charles: I'd thought about it before, so I presume yes.
Zois: "I presume." Did you want to kill him?
Charles: Yes, I guess I did. Yes, I did.

Such responses are not uncommon. I continuously pick up on Charles's defenses and point them out to him until he becomes aware of them and begins to make definitive statements.

Passivity and Helplessness. Adopting a passive stance is one way to avoid taking action, getting on with an issue, proceeding with your life. "I don't make enough money in my present job, but what can I do? I don't know any other kind of work." "I don't know" is a signal of helplessness. Someone who takes a helpless position might say, "I don't know what to do about my problem" or "I can't do anything about it." That person is really saying, "I'm not going to budge. I'm not going to change."

Passivity can mask both current and past emotions, particularly anger or deep pain or hurt. The fear of expressing the anger or grievance can be so great that doing nothing, as self-defeating as that is, seems preferable. The pain and hurt can be so intense that a lack of thought and action appears to be a better choice than coping with the problem.

If you have left anger unexpressed in the past, that pattern will continue in the present. You may mask current anger with passivity or helplessness. You may leave your grievances unaired, and over time, that may result in great harm to your relationships. We've seen the paralyzing effect that anger and his response to it—passivity—had on Charles.

The Emotional Defenses

Emotional defenses are emotions that are used, in an inauthentic or false manner, to mask underlying pain. The most common emotional defenses are weepiness, depression, and anger.

Weepiness. A common defense, weepiness is often used to hide deep anger and sometimes to mask pain and guilt. A father takes the car keys away from his son as a punishment, and the boy bursts into tears; but he's not sad or hurt—he's enraged at his father. Or a woman says, "Whenever my boss raises his voice, I start to cry." What she truly wants to do is grab him by the throat.

You're not always crying because you're sad. Sometimes people say, "I got so angry I cried." But such crying is not an expression of anger; it is a cover for it. Likewise, responding with tears to frustration, guilt, or anger is a way of avoiding these underlying emotions.

If you find yourself in tears, ask yourself if you are responding to sadness or grief. Instead, you may be reacting to a situation you perceive as frustrating because it is out of your control or to circumstances that cause you anger that you don't want to feel. Rather than a manifestation of authentic feelings of sadness, your tears may be a defense against other negative emotions.

Depression. Anger can be so intense that you can't tolerate it and, as a defense, you become depressed. The depression becomes a means of not dealing with angry emotions, because if you're overwhelmed by depression you are incapable of lashing out. You move, think, and speak slowly; all the resources of your psyche are depleted. You might have a hard time reading a newspaper or watching television; you lose interest in it or don't remember what's happened. You have a diminished desire for sex. You can't sleep at night, or, conversely, you sleep a lot. You avoid social activities.

If you're depressed, you lack spontaneity and show little concern for things you would normally care about— your finances, your personal appearance, the people and issues that interested and excited you in the past. You have vague physical complaints, such as pains and headaches, or thoughts of impending doom.

In this book, we're concerned with two kinds of depression. One is authentic depression, or grief: you suffer an important loss, you get fired, you break up with a spouse or a lover. In those situations, it's normal to feel sad—the grieving process is necessary and healthy.

On the other hand, when you use the vague depression that we call defensive, you claim to be depressed, and yet one day you are feeling fine and the next day you are depressed again. Defensive depression is a negative mood that people go in and out of; it is nonspecific and hard to catalog, because the symptoms are always somewhere out of reach. If you suffer from this type of moodiness, you may be using depression as a defense, and it may have more to do with you than with another person or your situation. Defensive depression is a common cover for anger and other deep emotions.

The distinction between grief and defensive depression is that defensive depression almost always has a self-devaluing quality. With grief, there is no self-devaluation; there's a sense of loss and an appropriate sadness, followed within a reasonable period of time by a resolution of the grief, in which the lost person or situation lives on within you. You can be enriched by the healthy resolution of a grieving experience, as opposed to the self-devaluing nature of depression, which gives rise to feelings of worthlessness or guilt.

It is sometimes difficult for depressed people to tell whether their depression is a defense. People usually don't see depression as a defense. They see it as something that descends on them—they suffer with it; it's out of their control. But this needn't be the case when the depression is a defense—indeed it shouldn't be the case if you're seeking emotional honesty and health. If you can't sort out your depression on your own, consider a professional consultation. If you make excuses for avoiding a consultation, you may be using your depression as a defense.

There are other kinds of depression that don't fall into the category of either grief or defensive depression. For a variety of reasons, including genetic causes, people suffer from severe depressions that require medication and sometimes hospitalization. In the section "Coping with Pain and Hurt" in Chapter 9, I comment on the use of medication in treating depression. However, this book doesn't include discussion of these severe depressions.

Anger. There are two kinds of anger. One is appropriate as a response to an attack or threat, and the other derives from internal psychic conflict, from a sense of hurt, insecurity, and inadequacy. This second kind of anger is defensive in nature. A way of feeling powerful temporarily, it tries to mask a sense of powerlessness.

Justifiable anger may be an appropriate emotion in a given situation, whereas defensive anger is a cover-up for deeper feelings. Just as weeping and one kind of depression can be used as a defense against anger, superficial anger can be used as a defense against sadness or pain, against grief, or against a feeling of having been cheated and victimized. It's often easier to show anger than to show hurt feelings.

I treat many people who are chronically angry. They complain, to the point of being enraged, about their fathers, mothers, husbands, or wives, when underneath the rage there is enormous pain. No matter how much energy they must expend to be angry, they find it easier to pay that price than to experience the underlying emotion, for to admit that someone has hurt you is to make yourself vulnerable. The trouble is that it is easier only in the short run, because failing to address them allows these troubling feelings to remain, draining your energy and resources.

One classic expression of defensive rage is displaced anger. A woman is fighting with her husband when their son comes home with the wrong dog food, and she blows her top. "What is it with you? How stupid can you get? I didn't want canned food; I wanted dry food. What does it take to make you understand?" Meanwhile she really wants to tell her husband what she thinks of him, but she doesn't.

One of my patients, Phil, told me this story: His wife had once again talked him into doing something he didn't want to do—fix the dining room chandelier on his day off. "I didn't feel like doing it that day, and I was having trouble getting a part to fit. I was mad and I said to her, 'For Christ's sake, would you get the hell away from the goddam ladder?'"

As we talked, Phil came to the realization that he felt intimidated by his wife. Rather than being direct and telling her she was making him feel powerless, his reaction was a defensive rage. He found it easier to express anger than to acknowledge painful feelings, but under the anger was his unspoken hurt. When he dealt directly with the issues, Phil's sense of powerlessness and victimization dissipated. As his frustration lessened, so did his anger.

It's important to distinguish between defensive anger and the appropriate, or authentic, anger that you may feel as a deep and strong emotion under appropriate circumstances. People often employ defenses against this type of anger. However, anger used as a defense is not an emotion, and you should not confuse defensive anger with authentic anger. Authentic anger is discussed further in Chapter 4, in the section "Anger: Who's at Risk?"

The Intellectual Defenses

Underlying emotions can be hidden by defenses that use the cognitive aspects of the psyche—the intellect. The intellectual defenses are based on a claim of objectivity. A person who says, "I'm being objective," is saying that his response is not colored by emotion. Claiming objectivity can be a way of defending against emotions.

The emotional defenses are tricky because they substitute one emotion for another, deeper one. The problem posed by the intellectual defenses is that by definition they avoid the emotions. People who use them provide layer upon layer of platitudes, excuses, and jargon that "explain" to their satisfaction their self-defeating patterns.

Rationalization. Perhaps the most common intellectual defense, rationalization, is making excuses. A straightforward defense, it means exactly what it says—that you give reasons to justify your unacceptable attitudes and types of behavior. Rationalizing is offering an alibi for why you didn't do what you were supposed to do, or for why you did what you shouldn't have done.

It also allows you to explain away the behavior of others. "He fired me, but what else could he do? He has a boss who's a son of a bitch, and he had no choice." In thinking about his father's anger with him on the day he died, a man tells himself, "Well, he was on a lot of medication.", But his rationalizing doesn't help the way he feels; he was still hurt by his father's behavior.

People often rationalize the use of the emotional defenses. You might say, "Of course I cried. I had every reason to." Such a comment brings up an important point: rationalizations frequently contain an element of truth or validity, but it's a mistake to focus on that validity rather than on the emotion that gave rise to the rationalization. There may indeed have been a reason to cry; the situation may have been painful or sad. But crying may not be the best way to handle the situation. Rationalizations work well because other people have a hard time arguing against statements that contain a kernel of truth, and they make the mistake of focusing on the valid part of a statement rather than on what the defensive person is trying to deny to himself.

Everyone rationalizes. It's one of the simplest defenses and one of the easiest to utilize. You don't have to do anything except react with a pat response that, unfortunately, doesn't address your real feelings.

Rationalizations are commonplace. We've all heard them, thought them, used them. The problem is that we believe them! If you want to be emotionally honest, you must look at such reactions in a new way, be critical of them, put them aside, and get down to the underlying issue—that you feel guilty, that you are afraid of becoming intimate with another person, that you fear your own anger—as painful and anxiety provoking as the process may be.

Intellectualization. Intellectualization is retreating into philosophy and using it as a substitute for doing something about what's bothering you. Unlike rationalization, which involves giving specific reasons or excuses for your behavior, intellectualization is a general, nonspecific way of viewing a situation.

People who intellectualize don't talk about themselves or the issue. For instance, "Man was meant to be alone" is a generalization about life that makes no specific comment on the situation at hand. Intellectualization is geared to inaction: "We were born to suffer" or "What is life about?" People who intellectualize use their thoughts to cover up their feelings.

I asked a patient, "How do you feel about your wife running off with your best friend?" His response: "Well, what is the human condition really? You can't expect much from other people. Shock and surprise are at every turn. That's life." No, that's intellectualization: an impersonal, philosophical way of coping with a painful situation. Intellectualization is a particularly useful defense for people who are mired in self-hatred. By keeping the focus general, they build a case for universal suffering.

The difficulty with intellectualizing is that even when the concept is valid, it doesn't make you feel better. Intellectualization is one of the therapist's stiffest challenges. Charles, the patient you met in Chapter 1, was a master at using intellectual defenses to remain walled off from his emotions.

Very often people defend against change by saying, "I know that I never get in touch with my feelings" or "I know that my problem is that I'm very angry about what happened with my brother on Thanksgiving." But that's just a description. Discussing problems in such terms is not really experiencing the emotions. Unfortunately, it is sometimes allowed to pass for productive activity; people in some types of therapy come away with a notion that this kind of intellectualization is evidence of improvement. But talking about issues is not a substitute for experiencing emotions and modifying the negative attitudes and behavior associated with them.

Avoidance. Staying away from situations that are emotionally painful is the defense of avoidance. It is commonly used against overwhelming feelings, such as anger. Frequently people confuse the avoidance of an emotion with the emotion itself: "I got so angry with him, I walked out of the room." But such a statement doesn't explain how angry you were; it explains what you did in response to your anger. Avoidance is a maneuver against coming to grips with just how angry or hurt you are.

One way to stay away from feelings is to stay away from people, to turn down invitations and not seek out other people. This type of avoidance is a way of defending against intimacy. Like rationalization, avoidance is commonplace because it is an easy defense to utilize. It is a passive activity that requires very little effort.

Avoidance can take indirect forms. For example, sarcasm is an effective way of keeping people away; most people don't want to be around someone who is often sarcastic. Such a person is most likely unhappy and wants to remain isolated in a private world of misery.

Denial. An insidious kind of defense, denying that you behave in a certain way or have certain feelings prevents internal or external dialogue: "I was not drunk. That cop was just looking for someone to arrest." Or "I do not get angry at home. If anything, I bend over backward to make my family happy."

People who use the defense of denial are often at odds with others' assessments of them; they are not open to what others have to say about them. When confronted with their tendency to deny, they characterize themselves, often with pride, as stubborn or hardheaded.

Because frequently these people suffer from the isolation of thought from emotion, the denial may be based on ignorance that the feelings exist. Some people use the defense of denial when they are confronted with the painful truth and there's no way to explain it away. Denial is the most straightforward way to avoid dealing with painful issues. Unfortunately, the result is that these people don't face the real issues that are disturbing them.

Projection. When on a deep level we sense something about ourselves that we don't want to face, we sometimes project, or thrust, that attitude or way of behaving away from ourselves. With projection, we attribute our unacceptable qualities to another person.

A man might say, "I really hate Stanley. He's so sloppy, and he treats his wife like dirt," when his real thought is that he's that way himself. He doesn't like having Stanley around because Stanley reminds him of his own worst qualities, which he'd rather not face.

A person who projects is overtly expressing mistrust of other people while attributing to them impulses that he may have himself. He says, "Where did my wife go tonight? Is she having an affair?" instead of acknowledging, "I find myself attracted to the woman in the next office." The father of a teenager says, "These young guys today, all they want to do is chase girls," when that's what he really wants to do; he covers it up by projecting.

Is It Ever Okay to Use Defenses?

Sometimes it is appropriate to be defensive. You can't go through life constantly using a glaring searchlight to illuminate the truth. There's usually no need to worry about using defenses in minor situations or when the implications aren't serious. For example, on a first date a woman is disappointed because the man seems insensitive, talking only about himself. She wants to give him the benefit of the doubt, so she rationalizes that he is nervous. However, if the relationship continues and the man's insensitivity persists, it would be inappropriate for her to make excuses for it and stay in an unsatisfactory relationship.

Defenses are also useful on a deeper level. Immediately after a death, separation, or other sudden loss, your feelings may be too raw to face. By using defenses, you may give yourself time to adjust to what has happened. But, just as you must at some point remove the bandage from a healing wound, so must you eventually bring out into the open the pain and conflict you feel at your loss.

Defenses are inappropriate when they prevent you from being as satisfied and happy with your life as you could be—for example, when you use defenses in recurring situations that cause you emotional discomfort; when you feel guilty about persistent feelings of anger; or when you have great anxiety about intimacy. Defenses are damaging when you use them to keep yourself isolated, unhappy, and alone.

How the Therapist Discovers the Patient's Defenses

Some defenses are easy to spot. For instance, whenever patients say "maybe" or "perhaps" or "I guess" or "I think," they're using the defense of vagueness; the therapist detects it because it's a qualified statement. It's also quite easy to identify rationalization, intellectualization, and denial.

You don't have to be a psychiatrist to recognize these simple defenses. All you need are definitions of the terms. However, within the context of a therapy session, the therapist must keep strictly focused on the fact that a rationalization, for instance, is not an appropriate response, especially when the question is very specific.

For example, I may ask, "What is your emotion right now as you tell me you didn't get a raise?" I'm not asking for your views on the national economy. I don't want an account of how you're not going to be able to move into a nicer apartment, nor do I want to hear about your car payments. I'm asking about your emotion. I asked a very straightforward question. There's only one appropriate answer: you say you feel happy, sad, angry, elated, depressed, or some other emotion. It's that simple. If you do not answer the question directly, you are utilizing a defense.

But what about the emotional defenses? It is easier to identify the non-emotional defenses—rationalization, intellectualization, and so forth—than to identify the emotional defenses. In dealing with the latter, the therapist must judge whether the weepiness, depression, or anger is justified. For example, a man expresses anger about being stood up for a date. There's a certain validity to that anger, but the emotion that is more intense and more destructive to him is the sense of hurt that he doesn't want to acknowledge either to himself or to the therapist. He finds it easier to talk about being angry than to face the deeper feeling.

An emotional defense is more difficult to deal with because the person focuses on the aspect of the emotion that is justified or causes the least psychic discomfort. It's not that the anger doesn't exist; the point is that the patient is using it defensively to avoid acknowledging hurt, painful feelings. The therapist must identify the defensive nature of the anger and probe past it to the underlying feelings.

Often when a therapist points to anger as defensive, it's obvious that linked to the anger are other emotions, such as hurt and pain. It's a little more difficult to detect the difference between true sadness and defensive depression or weepiness that is used as a defense, as a wall of tears between patient and therapist. In scrutinizing depression, I don't rely solely on responses to my probing. My determination is also based on my understanding of what I've learned about the patient and the way the patient deals with emotions and defenses in general.

One woman cried throughout the evaluation session. Some of her tears were justified and others weren't. At one point she wept while talking about the suicide of her mother; at other times, she was worried about how I was going to feel about her; and she erupted into tears when recounting a disagreement she had had with her husband about finances. The latter two simply didn't ring true as causes for tearfulness. The therapist's determination is based on a combination of content and context.

How to Know When You're Being Defensive

If you overuse defenses, perhaps you are avoiding the important issues in your life. If you spend your time rationalizing your unhappiness or avoiding other people, at the end of your life you may not have much to show for it. You may have kept yourself away from intimate relationships or from work that would have made you happy. You may have missed many of the opportunities that life offers.

Relying on defenses isn't the only way to deal with painful memories and emotions. Instead of avoiding the fact that you feel guilty or angry or that you're in pain, you can bring these memories and emotions to the surface, grapple with them, and lessen the pain and problems they cause in your life. It is important to keep in mind that a given defense might be covering up more than one problem, or that you might be using two or more defenses at once to mask a painful emotion or impulse.

Think about how you might be using the defenses discussed in this chapter. Choose, from your past or your present life, a situation that you consider significant and that caused you to have a reaction or response. Write, first, a brief description of the situation and, second, your response.

Now test that response by answering the following two questions:

1. How did you feel in response to the situation you described? Did you respond by describing an emotion?

Instead of an emotion, did you describe something else? Did you describe the situation? Did you make a philosophical observation? Did you deny that you had an emotion? Did you explain what you did about your emotion without describing it? If so, you used a defense and, after reading this chapter, you can probably identify which one.

If your response was not a description ("I walked away" or "I started to cry" or "I thought, What's the use?") but an emotion, then you are not being defensive.

2. If your response to the situation you described was anger or sadness, you must now judge the appropriateness of that emotion. Is it justifiable, or have you used the trappings of anger or sadness in order to block a deeper and truer response that you are reluctant to acknowledge?

Strict self-monitoring is required in detecting emotional defenses. Try to probe below the first level of your response to discover deeper feelings that may exist. Objectify the situation: ask yourself whether, if another person reported the same situation and a response similar to yours, you would find anger or depression justifiable, or whether another emotion might be suggested.

What Happens When the Defenses Are Lifted?

A defense is designed to protect, but it's similar to the caring of an overly cautious parent, who can provide so much protection that the child never becomes capable of living an independent life.

To gain happiness and satisfaction, you must put aside your defenses, as you once put aside the games of childhood. Becoming an adult means taking responsibility, living an autonomous life, and relating on an equal footing with other human beings. When that happens at home, at work, and with other people, you live a freer and happier existence.

The transition from childhood to adulthood is sometimes painful, and so is the transition from a life that is encumbered by defenses to one that is free of them. To make that transition, you must suffer the pain of dealing with the real feelings that you've been burying.

Shedding your defenses is liberating. Once you have eliminated or modified them, you can face the troubling feelings you have been avoiding. Such confrontations, which are more difficult in the anticipation than in the doing, provide for emotional honesty and clarity, and they allow you to achieve intimacy and productive relationships with those around you. Finally, with the ability to be intimate comes the opportunity to derive a maximum of satisfaction and richness from your life.

Here are the defenses represented by your reactions to questions in the miniquiz that began this chapter:

- *You've put on some weight:* a. denial; b. anger; c. depression; d. no defense.
- *Argument with your brother:* a. avoidance; b. helplessness; c. projection; d. no defense.

- *No promotion:* a. intellectualization; b. anger, rationalization, and denial; c. avoidance; d. no defense.
- *Sister hurts your feelings:* a. avoidance; b. rationalization; c. anger; d. no defense.

CHAPTER 4

Your Buried Feelings: Hidden But Not Silenced

"What went wrong? It should have been different. What was I thinking?" Such thoughts haunt us when our relationships and endeavors turn into spoiled opportunities, misadventures, and bruised feelings.

"What was I trying to prove? Why didn't I know better?" The answers lie hidden deep in our personalities.

There is within each of us a psychic engine driven in part by strong feelings of anger, hurt, and guilt. We hide these painful feelings from the world because we perceive them to be too dangerous to acknowledge. Often we even hide them from ourselves.

Like everyone else, you are often ashamed or fearful when you have strong emotions. Such feelings make you uncomfortable, as do the memories of what caused them and the impulses to which they give rise. As a result, you hide negative feelings, memories, and impulses from your awareness by burying them and hoping they will go away. You try to be happy with the false idea that if you don't think about something it must not be there.

Your everyday conversation and behavior incorporate defenses that act as a cover for your negative emotions. Nevertheless, those emotions make themselves known by transmitting covert messages. You seem to be saying one thing, but the message you convey is different from the meaning your words express. You may not hear the underlying statements you make about yourself, but other people do.

Sometimes your hidden negative feelings are valid and based in a historical or emotional reality, and sometimes they are not. Regardless of their exact makeup and origin, they decide your success or failure more than any other element in your life. These private, subjective feelings about yourself and other people help determine the quality of your relationships with family, friends, and lovers. They influence your success at work and your reaction to a loss. When you have a problem that you cannot seem to solve, the fears and anxieties generated by your negative emotions and impulses prompt you to speak and behave in ways that intensify that problem.

Such feelings are not foreign influences that enter and dominate your psyche. They are rooted in and sustained by the events of your past and your memories of those events. These feelings determine your attitudes and behavior in a way that's so automatic and natural you don't know it exists.

The problems and pain, the losses and changes that life brings, will naturally generate deep feelings. Anger, hurt, and guilt are normal initial responses to stress, but that is not an excuse to perpetuate them indefinitely and to lead a failed existence.

Understanding your hidden emotions and impulses will help eliminate the question "Where did I go wrong?" Facing your strongest emotions will help you resolve such problems as self-sabotage, loneliness, and interpersonal problems. You'll be able to see how you have been standing in your own way and why you haven't been able to deal effectively with people and situations.

Changing your life will not require you to accept a new philosophy, but it will require you to understand the part of yourself you've been avoiding. Once you have come face to face with the emotions you've buried, they will stop silently controlling you, and they'll stop throwing up invisible hurdles for you to trip over. You will be able to live a life directed by a personality that is free rather than manipulated by covert feelings.

The "Prehistoric" You

Your individual psychic engine—the sum total of your memories, feelings, and impulses—defines your personal, subjective sense of being in the world. It is tailor-made for you by your past experiences and interactions. Its author is your past relationships, dating back to your earliest days. It originated in a period of your past that is beyond recall—the precognitive period, the time before you could know or understand.

Reason, or the ability to organize experiences in a context that we can understand and interpret, is one of two key elements that makes us cognitive, or knowing, individuals. The other is language, which provides the symbols of those interpretations and which emotionally colors experience. In the first months of our existence we are unable to put order to events and stimuli because we have not yet developed the ability to reason and to use language.

Nevertheless, this precognitive period is replete with responses that form the matrix of your emotional self. Without reason and without language, the precognitive experience is a purely emotional one—it is emotions superimposed on physiological needs. How you experience being in the world at this time forever exists within you, but it remains beyond the realm of what you can know about yourself.

The emotions of that "prehistoric" and unknowable period fall into two categories: the positive emotions, when we experience a sense of harmony and well-being, when we receive nourishment or stimulation that contributes to our survival and development; and the negative emotions, when nurturing and stimulation are denied. The dark side of the precognitive period awakens within us the possibility of our annihilation. For infants, who depend totally on other people for their continued existence, the potential for annihilation is a reality, one that they discern not logically but emotionally. This emotional experience of chaos and panic forms the basis for the fears and anxieties of the logical, reasoning adult who is to come.

Throughout your life your early pleasant experiences are your barometer for whether you are in harmony with your world. As you mature, the things and situations you need in order to feel content become more numerous and more complex. Yet, no matter how complicated your desires may appear, you are essentially seeking a replica of the emotional well-being you experienced during the precognitive period of your life.

What you are left with from your infancy is an emotional sense that is ineffable. You have experienced the emotions, yet you cannot communicate their substance to another person. Anyone who has tried to relate the emotional tone of a dream has had this experience. To use another analogy, explaining an emotion from the precognitive period is similar to attempting to describe a primary color.

The feelings that make you who you are—the positive memories, emotions, and impulses as well as the negative ones—give you your own individual humanity, which is something that therapy or any corrective experience cannot take away from you. One reason for this is that fundamental

elements of your emotional construct were assembled during a period before your ability to reason. As a result, a
thorough knowledge of the makeup of that construct is
beyond your reach.

What does all this mean to you as you strive for emotional change? Your experiences during the precognitive
period explain why you still resonate somewhat with certain
emotions from the past even after you've gone through a
successful therapy, after you've read this book, after you've
undergone any curative experience. You still experience
certain dreams, still have difficulty with certain key figures
and issues in your life. This does not mean you have not
made progress. You can lessen your confusion and frustration by accepting that this period will always affect you but
that you can never recall or analyze it.

During therapy your emotions and impulses become
attenuated, or minimized, rather than eradicated. Therapy
does not produce automatons and robots. It simply helps
you do an inventory and bring into balance the conflicting
emotions, impulses, and experiences that make up the
sum total of who you are. Your negative emotions and
impulses do not go away completely, because a fundamental
part of your emotional makeup is beyond your ability to
know.

Anger: Who's at Risk?

The primal experience of anger was useful, and perhaps essential, to our ancestors ten thousand years ago.
Over the millennia, however, the need for aggressive action
has been modified and channeled. Although there is still a
great deal of primitive behavior in the world, today anger is
not so much essential as inevitable. It is part of the genetic
makeup of all human beings, and it is going to be elicited
from time to time. Yet, as strong as the emotion of anger

can be, you needn't fear it or experience it in a way that is harmful rather than productive for you.

Defensive anger is unjustified or exaggerated rage that serves to mask another feeling. But some anger is justified. When you are attacked, for example, and you need to defend yourself, profound instinctual impulses toward self-protection arise in you. Anger is generally considered justifiable when a person is assaulted or seriously threatened.

When the need for anger is perceived accurately and when it is expressed appropriately, anger can lead to behavior that deals constructively with the source of a perceived threat. However, frequently your anger is colored and distorted by your past experiences. An event in the present can remind you of a similar one in the past, and your response can be an echo of your past emotion rather than a new emotion based on the present. For example, an abusive boss may remind you of your abusive father, and your reaction may be to your father rather than to your boss.

Anger can also cause problems when you cannot feel your anger or when you fail to express it appropriately, and you instead let it become a dominating part of your personality. (The fear of your own anger and the angry victim role are both discussed further in Chapter 5.)

Some people are uncomfortable with their anger because they fear what they will do to others if it goes out of control. However, they rationalize just the opposite: "If I become angry, something bad will happen to me." This defense prevents them from even beginning to face their true anxiety about their rage and, more important, the past events that molded this attitude. Charles, you will remember, realized during his first therapy session that his suppressed anger derived from his overwhelming rage fantasies.

Often people are unaware of the appropriate way to express anger. They equate verbalizing angry thoughts and feelings with acting on them. People who fear their own anger generally don't realize that expressing anger doesn't mean they have to explode in a fit of rage. A simple statement—"I'm angry with you for breaking our date" or "I'm upset with the way you treated me"—can be an appropriate way to let people know you are angry with them.

If you're unable to express your anger appropriately, it may become obscured by a sense of being cheated and perennially victimized, by a misplaced sense of guilt, by such defenses as passivity and avoidance, or even by displaced or defensive anger.

When you become angry with someone close to you, you may have a hard time putting that anger aside. You can't deal with it in the same way you would deal with a rude taxi driver. Why? If it was a pure emotion—anger and only anger—you would have no trouble expressing it and then quickly putting it behind you. But because of the nature of a relationship, pain and hurt are involved, keeping you engaged in a negative way. If you want to understand anger in relationships, you also have to understand pain and hurt.

When it comes to relationships we tend to focus primarily on anger when we're really feeling more hurt than anger. It's easier to ventilate anger at somebody, to feel victimized and cheated, than it is to acknowledge hurt and pain, which means admitting that you're vulnerable, that you have run the risk of being close to someone and suffered as a result.

If people leave you, you feel a blow to your ego and self-esteem—you're not worthy, they prefer somebody else, they'd rather be alone than with you. In a similar way, when people lose their jobs, retire, suffer serious financial reversals, or undergo important changes in their lives, they may feel a devaluation of their self-image. The defensive anger that erupts in response to these experiences masks the underlying hurt and pain.

Hurt: Feelings of Pain and Sadness

Experiencing emotional pain—being hurt by people—is inevitable. When loved ones die, the thought of not seeing and being with them again can seem too much to bear. Similarly, when someone you love rejects or abandons you, you are hurt to the core. When you lose your job or when your children leave home, you may suffer a devastating blow to your self-image, feeling nothing but the pain and thinking your life can never be the same.

Abandonment, separation, and loss are insults to the psyche, because they make it struggle with the belief that it deserves to be left behind, that it is not entitled to anything else. In other words, pain and hurt imply devaluation. Being abandoned or rejected can suggest that you deserve to be left behind because you are worthless or inadequate.

If you are rejected, you may start to believe that you deserve to be rejected, and this can cause problems for you. However, if you refuse to believe this demeaning message, or if you accept it only in part, then you can turn your back on the person who hurt you and eliminate or at least reduce the pain.

The greatest threat that pain and hurt pose is the possibility that you will accept the hurtful messages as true. When you accept the notion that you are of little value, when you take rejection as a judgment in which you concur, a sense of being victimized can dominate your life. But when you refuse to accept the message that you are inadequate and worthless, the pain will gradually lessen and take its place among your life experiences.

If you remember your father as judgmental, and if that memory is accompanied by a feeling of anger or a sense of victimization, then, in whole or in part, you believe that you are worthy of a negative judgment. Otherwise you'd be able to view his attitude within a more balanced perspective. You'd be able to say, "What a pity Dad could see only people's shortcomings, including mine." But when you think of your father's attitude toward you and at the same time feel a visceral emotion of pain or sadness, you're hooked on the notion that you are not worthy of anything more than what you believe Dad thought about you. Without that belief, there's no psychic conflict.

Franz Kafka intuited this emotional dynamic. In a long letter to his father, he laid out all the issues that were wrong in their relationship. Near the end of the letter, which he never sent, Kafka says that he knows what his father's response will be. He will say, "In this as in everything else you have proved to me that all my reproaches were justified, and that one especially justified charge was still missing: namely, the charge of insincerity, obsequiousness, and parasitism." In reply, Kafka states, "Not even your mistrust of others is as great as my self-mistrust, which you have bred in me."

Likewise, Kafka's story "The Metamorphosis" is about a man, Gregor Samsa, who so strongly accepts his family's negative judgment of him that he turns into an insect and is swept out with the garbage. Gregor supported his mother and father and sister, but, as dependent people often do, they resented him and showed irritation at their dependence even as they accepted its benefits. Because he knew he was guilty of stifling them, of standing in the way of their independence and self-satisfaction, Gregor concurred in their judgment; he saw mirrored in their eyes his own self-hate. One reason Kafka's writings have universal appeal is that the potential for self-devaluation exists within each of us.

An overextended period of mourning is said to be pathological—or unhealthy—because it is too long and too intense. But it's not only in a mourning process that such an extended, intense reaction can occur. Some people who suffer abandonment or rejection are forever changed; some never recover from the loss of a spouse through death or divorce.

Pain and hurt are a condition of life that no one escapes. Problems arise when these emotions become a threat to accomplishing intimacy. When you feel the pain of disappointment or rejection, you may find that anger, avoidance, or another defense will naturally arise to block the pain. Your anger may be justified; someone may have indeed betrayed you. Your avoidance is understandable; you don't want to be hurt again. But your ability to take action—either to reconstitute the relationship, to have a balanced view of it, or, if necessary, to put it behind you—is directly related to your continued capacity for intimacy.

Guilt: How to Be Your Own Worst Friend

Everyone feels guilt, which may be rooted either in the perception of wrongdoing or in actual wrongdoing.

As we live and work together we constantly try to get along with one another, with varying degrees of success. Things could always have been done or said differently. We don't always do what's right. Because people are not perfect, guilt is a normal response to many situations. That's why, when we lose someone or a situation changes, feelings of guilt frequently arise.

Doing wrong—whether we call it sin or, as the ancient Greeks did, "missing the mark"—is part of living in the world. You cannot avoid it all the time. Nor can you live without experiencing the impulse to act out negative or petty attitudes toward others.

Guilt encourages a sense of lack of entitlement. It tells an individual, "Because your father went to his grave a lonely, isolated, miserable human being and you contributed to that situation, you are guilty. You are not entitled to a happy, successful, fulfilled life." This sense of lack of entitlement can give rise to self-sabotage.

You may not feel guilt directly. Instead, you may engage

in self-sabotage and be left with the mute testimony of the underlying hatred you feel toward yourself: failed careers, loneliness, lost relationships, and sometimes, in the face of success in those areas, a sense of inner desperation you don't understand.

Guilt may stem from a misperception of your aggressive and negative impulses. You may see your actions as more threatening or damaging than they actually were. You may wrongly but firmly believe that you have betrayed those who love you, that you have let people down or harmed them.

Similarly, you may impose your values about how life should be lived on someone else and then suffer because that person doesn't conform to your values. "My mother lives in this little apartment, and I feel so guilty about the way she's living." But maybe Mom likes the little apartment, for whatever reason. You like sprawling lawns and views of horses out your back window, so you think Mom should, too. But she hates horses! She wants to have a little dog in a one-room apartment. You may be suffering from artificial guilt, worrying that your mother is not living according to your values, when you're really denying her the right to live the life she wants to lead, and you're punishing yourself in the process.

Some people who suffer from self-pity embrace guilt and indulge in it chronically. They feel warmed by the glow of the thought that they didn't do the right thing. They perceive their guilt as an atonement, a kind of self-flagellation. A woman cries for her father who was sick for years, but she's not crying for Dad; she's crying for herself. More than that, she's assuming the mantle of guilt because it fits nicely over her sense of self-pity.

But what if you do have something to feel guilty about? Maybe you did ignore your children because you were so caught up in your career. Maybe you had affairs that deeply hurt your spouse. It's not helpful to rationalize: "It wasn't my fault" or "I didn't really mean it." You have to face the reality of what you did. The hallmark of mental health is being able to look at a situation—in all of its aspects and with all of its pain and failure—and to say at the end, "That's the way it was." Does that mean "To hell with it"? No, it means you can learn a lesson from the experience and carry on.

My patient John suffered with guilt, believing that his father's struggle to put him through college had hastened his death. The young man tortured himself with thoughts of what he hadn't done: he could have worked nights and done more for himself, instead of going out with his friends; he did not express enough gratitude to his father. In truth, the father did work hard for John, and maybe he would have lived longer if John had not gone to school or had worked part-time. Perhaps John could have shown more gratitude. What can he do in response to his feeling that he shortchanged his father?

With some problems, there is only so much you can accomplish therapeutically. Guilt is one of those problems. If you feel guilty, you must move past your defenses and make a clear assessment of your perception of recalled events. Then you must evaluate and experience the emotions generated by your memories, and defuse the impulses that have arisen from them. But what happens when, after all is said and done, you're left with an incontrovertible truth: Dad was cheated, or Mom died alone because of something you did. What do you do now?

The answer to that question is not a psychiatric or a therapeutic one. Attempting to apply psychiatric calculus to a situation of actual wrongdoing is not going to work. The question now becomes "How do you deal with having done wrong? How do you live with guilt?"

All of us owe the past, whether it's people or circumstances, and we can "pay" that debt by helping others. Years ago I had to take some science courses in another city, and a friend of mine made arrangements for me to stay at his house. I offered to pay rent, but he said he wouldn't accept money from me. When I protested, he said that someday I would be in a position to help another person, and that help would be my payment to him. That concept had a lasting effect on me.

John may see ways that he can help someone else in his journey through life. If John's father was as good a man as John thinks he was, he would be happy that his son is helping others. Such actions become a way for him to pay back the debt to his father.

As a separate point, did John do anything to make his father happy while he was alive, or was John a total monster? Surely he was not a monster. Relationships always contain a mixture of positive and negative elements.

The goal is to learn from our mistakes and carry on. Would John's father want him to be rooted in guilt, punishing and sabotaging himself? That's very unlikely, and it would be selfish of John to do that. His guilt would become more important than his love for his father, compounding his original error. John would betray his father's memory by punishing himself.

If you look at your life in perspective, you'll see that no relationship is without its imperfection, its guilt, its stress and strain—that's the human condition. If you want to be rooted in guilt about what you did to your father or your mother or someone else you loved, you can do that. Or you can acknowledge that all of us are guilty in one way or another.

But then we must say, I did these things; what about it? What came out of it? Did anything good come from it? What can I do to make it different? Can anything good come from it?

Your Emotions Color Your Memories

We've already discussed how your recollections of the past can never be complete because as an infant you experienced strong emotions but hadn't yet developed reason and language. The emotional matrix that was formed during the precognitive period influences your feelings and reactions in a way that is impervious to your adult reasoning mind. In other words, the unknowable past colors your present.

But that's not the only reason to question your perceptions of the past. When you recall an event that took place years ago, there are often gaps in your memory and a vagueness about the remembered event. Your current feelings—including the strong negative ones you think you have hidden—fill in those gaps and clarify that vagueness with the emotional tone of the present. The feelings of today are laid over your memories of the past, blurring their accuracy. Many of the emotions you attach to such memories actually belong to the present.

As an adult of forty you may look back on something that happened to you at age five. That memory is colored by many of the experiences and emotions you have had from that time forward, so that the present is a prism through which you view the emotions of the past. The recalled event is actually an emotional composite of thirty-five years.

Many people have morbid mind-sets about relationships or events in their past. Such bleak perceptions very often result from the mechanics of distorted recall rather than from an objective account of the event.

A woman remembers how her father struggled to support the family, working in his shoe repair shop for a few pennies a day. While listening to her story, the therapist detects the influence of hidden negative emotions long before the patient becomes aware of them. Those emotions say to her: "You are not entitled to live a happy, successful, productive life because your father led a miserable one and you contributed to that misery." Her memory is permeated by a sadness and guilt that may or may not be justified, but she lives with this heavy burden, makes her decisions, and forms her relationships based on these painful recollections.

This woman feels that she wasn't sufficiently grateful to her father for his hard work, that she let him down. Her guilt derives from a mind-set that she has created over the years and that may or may not be accurate. It is not a result of her actual behavior toward her father. Her perception comes not only from that time as a child when she observed her dad but also from what her father represented for her as an adult and from her memory of him before he died. The essence of that early memory comes as much from the present as it does from her childhood.

Complicating the situation further, the experience of the child is colored by the child's own set of perceptions, real or imagined. At age five, the patient already had feelings about who her parents were and the impact she was having on their lives. So even the validity of her emotion at that time is in question. This is not a new concept. In *The Concluding Unscientific Postscript*, Kierkegaard delineated the proposition that all truth is subjective—an important point to keep in mind as you consider the emotions you attach to your recollections of past events.

There are two elements involved in a perception: the object or event observed and the observer's perceptive capabilities. The interaction of the two gives birth to the experience. However, what we perceive is limited by our ability to perceive it. We all know what an orange looks like. But if our vision were more acute, we could see the structure of the rind, and if it were extremely acute we could see the atoms and the molecules that make up the rind. Our perception of the orange is limited by our visual apparatus. In the same way, our ability to communicate what we perceive is limited by the restrictive nature of language.

In recalling important events in our past, it is easy to misperceive, and we should question our perceptions. We must look again and try to view old things in a new way. If she would suspend or look beyond her perceptions, the guilty woman might find herself thinking, "My father worked twelve hours a day, but that shop was always full of people kibitzing and shooting the breeze. Dad did work hard, and money was always tight, but although we lived in modest circumstances, there were times when we had a lot of fun. Dad was always short of money, but there were also nice things that went on. I always looked at that shop as fraught with struggle and frustration, but maybe that's not all there was to it."

Clarifying issues from the past does not mean coming to a conclusion about what's objectively accurate or inaccurate. But what do you rely on in emotional matters, since you can't rely on objectivity? What's important is identifying the emotions in the present that are linked to particular past events. As you're doing this, you must develop the ability to tolerate and work within your emotions while understanding that their appropriateness is in question.

Taking your perceptions at face value—whether you do it yourself or an ineffective therapist encourages you to do so—is certain to subvert a process of emotional change.

The Link between Your Defenses and Your Emotions

In your everyday life, your emotions and defenses run together like film that is speeded up, and you, like most people, can't follow the action. I want to slow down the film so that you will see the patterns and the action in your emotional life.

Even though the defenses sound straightforward, they can be insidious because they work so well together. In your everyday life they often join forces. Avoidance and rationalization are easily linked, as are avoidance and depression, projection and defensive anger, and many others. The defenses become mutual boosters, one effortlessly feeding the other.

Because your defenses and your hidden emotions are linked, you must stop and sift them out if you are to understand how they operate in your emotional life. Such sifting is a painstaking, time-consuming task, but it's worth the effort, particularly when an emotion and a defense become confused, as can happen with depression and anger. It's always vital to distinguish a true emotion from a defense.

A man named Frank came to me because he suffered from depression and he didn't know why. The current circumstances of his life were happy; he and his wife, who formerly had a drinking problem, had recently gotten their marriage back on a sound footing when she joined Alcoholics Anonymous and he joined a support group. Yet Frank was so depressed that he was putting no energy into his work, and on weekends he generally just slept or watched TV.

In speaking about the past and his wife's bouts of heavy drinking, Frank recalled a night when she got drunk, they quarreled, and she stormed out of the house:

Frank: She got into the car and drove off, and there was no way she should have been on the road in her condition.

Zois: What were your feelings?

Frank: Fear! Worry! I really expected that she would be killed in an accident.

Zois: In your mind what would she have looked like if she had died in an auto wreck?

Frank: (Upset) I can't talk about that.

Zois: You have a lot of feelings about that question.

Frank: Why do you want me to talk about that?

Zois: You haven't told me how you feel that I ask you to describe her dead.

Frank: (Still upset) No... I can't discuss that. I don't want to look at that!

Zois: You don't want to share your thoughts with me.
You want to keep a distance.

Frank: It makes me realize how angry I was with her.

Zois: How did your anger make you feel?

Frank: Ashamed. I love my wife, and I knew it was the
booze that was making her act so stupid. What
a creep I am.

Frank had become highly resistant to my line of questioning. My shift to a discussion of intimacy ("You don't
want to share your thoughts with me") is designed to lower
his defenses and elicit relevant emotionally charged material. Focusing on the issue of intimacy is the most effective
way to deal with highly resistant individuals and to ensure a
successful completion of treatment for all patients. The
maneuver bore fruit: Frank got past his defenses to acknowledge his angry feelings.

I used a particular technique in asking Frank detailed
questions about his wife dying in a car crash. I focused on
that fantasy because it was what he was suffering from: in
his mind he was a murderer; he had wanted her dead. As with
Charles in Chapter 1, I wanted Frank to be in touch with his
anger, to experience it in an immediate way in the session.

More than that, my questions enabled Frank to arrive at
a balanced view of his feelings toward his wife. His responses related not only his anger but also the sorrow and
guilt he felt as he imagined her death. As he became aware
of his other emotions Frank was able to move past his angry,
aggressive feelings to tender feelings; he was able to see
both. He could then make an appropriate inventory of the
complexity of his reaction rather than be left with a one-
sided view of it.

In his anger that night when his wife drove off, Frank's
negative emotions and fantasies came rushing over him. It all
happened so quickly that he couldn't separate his defenses
from his emotions; he couldn't see that he had covered his
angry fantasy with a rationalized concern, nor could he see

that his anger had left him with a burden of guilt. He later became depressed to mask the guilt he felt because a part of him had wished that his wife would die.

When Frank was able to view his feelings more clearly and to separate one from the other, he acknowledged the depth of his anger at his wife, and he realized how guilty that anger made him feel. When he got in touch with his tender feelings toward her and resolved his conflicts, he no longer needed his defensive depression and it disappeared.

Facing Your Hidden Feelings

"They're in my way. I'll never get anywhere because of them." "Who needs them?" "They're jealous." "Don't worry, I'll show them."

The famous "they" are at it again. Once more "they" have deprived you of a promotion, a piece of property you wanted to buy, a month in the country, the man or woman of your dreams. It's amazing what "they" can do. Of course, "they" actually reside between your ears. "They" are often a projection of a sense of inadequacy and lack of confidence generated by your most painful emotions and impulses and the defenses you erect to hide from them.

Getting in touch with your hidden feelings means making a simple acknowledgment—for example, that you are angry—and arriving at an understanding of what that means. This process involves clearing away your illusions and delusions about anger—that it's homicidal, that it's going to destroy you and others, that it will result in loss and abandonment. These are old wives' tales.

Many people believe that happiness occurs spontaneously, that when they wake up in the morning they're either happy or sad by accident. "I got up on the wrong side of the bed" implies that emotions come upon us for reasons that are unknown and leave us in a similar way. We don't treat them as part of the self; we treat them as pleasant or unpleasant visitors that come and go.

The ancient Greek concept of virtue is the willingness to do that which you can do to the best of your ability. The Greek concept of sin is missing the mark. These two ideas constitute useful parameters for a meditation on happiness, on being in harmony with your world—*your* world, not someone else's.

People don't critically examine the idea of happiness. We don't say, "I deserve to be happy. I need to be happy, to have a sense of well-being. I need to have my expectations understood, if not fulfilled. I don't want to live a life in which I set goals that are doomed to failure. I don't want to experience feelings of discontent and anger and victimization. I want to live in harmony with my world, so that I can do what I'm able to do."

In facing our most painful emotions, we are striving for a synchrony with our personal environment, a concept that is central to Eastern philosophy, which delineates the search for inner harmony. In the Western world, the ancients discussed that quest, but modern philosophy has turned instead to epistemology, the mechanics of knowing and understanding. One result is that in our culture we don't think in terms of striving for inner peace, which has become a concept like the weather: we talk about it but don't really think there's much we can do about it. We expect it to happen in the way that young people—and those not so young—expect romantic love automatically to lead to a successful ongoing relationship.

Inner harmony is viewed as some kind of chemical reaction that's suddenly going to happen—through therapy or association with a person or organization—and then turn into a perpetual motion machine that will continue without the infusion of any additional energy. That's not the case. As with anything else of value, a sense of personal equilibrium requires continuous work and effort.

If you don't confront your hidden and painful feelings, your life is likely to proceed at a less than optimal level of happiness. Your expectations become lowered, and your feelings remain constricted and inhibited. You relationalize or deny or avoid or become increasingly passive. It's like driving around in a car that's not tuned up; even though it knocks and rattles, you're happy that it runs at all. You're in a broken-down vehicle that you call your life, and for one reason or another you're happy to just clunk along.

A further danger is that you can sink into an unhealthy mind-set—of anger, of guilt, of hurt—that becomes an ingrained way of looking at the world. People trapped in such mind-sets say that they are paralyzed, burdened, locked in to attitudes, because they don't understand where they came from. But that argument denies the existence of choice. We can all choose to look beneath the surface and into that part of the psyche that holds our hidden emotions. If you can't make that choice, then you really are not functional, not a candidate for reading this book or doing this therapy. You need someone to be your warden, to take you around and make sure you feed yourself. However, if you're able to navigate through life, then you are also able to draw on your resources—to make choices, to take action.

In small doses, defenses are appropriate for getting through the day; in larger doses, they are not appropriate for getting through life. The same can be said about the strong and painful emotions that we sometimes bury: they are proper and appropriate in their place and in their time, but in order to achieve harmony with your personal universe you have to face them and then move past them.

When you ignore your deep emotions and rely on your defenses, you act in ways that can be destructive to you and to the people you love. When you cast off your defenses and face your painful feelings, you begin to get what you want out of life—out of your love relationships, your friendships, your work. That process seldom forces you to discover deep, dark, terrible secrets. You will probably find that the fears and anxieties that have been burdening your life were normal reactions to everyday events. Beyond that, you will see that you can work through and manage the emotions and impulses you have been avoiding. Facing your buried feelings is like turning on the light in a dark room and finding out that there never was a phantom there after all.

Trying to avoid painful emotions, memories, and impulses is, in any case, futile, because you're experiencing the guilt, anger, or pain anyway—for example, by drinking too much, by being absent from work, by arguing with people, or by other self-sabotaging behavior—even if you don't link your behavior with your underlying troubling emotions.

As uncomfortable as it may be initially, coming face to face with your anger, guilt, and pain results in great relief and freedom. Instead of being trapped in a morass of self-defeat, you will be in a position to explore and resolve your problems.

A Beginning Profile of Your Hidden Feelings

Begin to get acquainted with your hidden emotions by responding to the questions below. Answer "rarely or never," "sometimes," or "often," and rate each question 1, 2, or 3, according to this scale:

1. Rarely or never
2. Sometimes
3. Often

Your Feelings of Anger

1. Do you harbor prolonged resentment when you feel you've been treated badly?
2. After a threatening situation has passed, do you have fantasies of responding in a more forceful way than you did?
3. Do you scream and yell when things go wrong?

4. Does the thoughtlessness of another person make you angry?
5. Are you afraid of what you might do if you became angry?
6. After you get angry, do you feel guilty?
7. Do you hesitate to let people know when they've made you angry?
8. When you get angry, do you feel that your rage controls you rather than you controlling it?
9. Do you react angrily before you've thought about whether a person or situation is actually threatening you?
10. Do you have problems accepting an apology?

Tally your points and evaluate your score as follows:

10–14: If your answers are honest, you probably don't have a problem with anger.

15–22: You should give further consideration to the role of anger in your life.

23–30: You may be carrying a burden of anger that you should come to terms with.

Your Feelings of Hurt

1. Do you think of yourself as having a delicate or fragile ego?
2. When someone close to you lets you down, do you feel that you're to blame?
3. Do you accept rejection as something that you deserve?
4. When a parent or spouse criticizes you, do you take the criticism to heart?
5. When someone dies or an important circumstance of your life changes, does it take you a long time to get over it?

6. Do you feel it's best to let others make decisions and to let your feelings be known afterward?
7. Do you prefer to spend time on your own rather than risk potentially hurtful interactions with others?
8. Do you feel comfortable with feelings of disappointment?
9. Do you think of yourself as a victim?
10. Are you reluctant to think about how you may have contributed to a situation that hurt you?

Tally your points and evaluate your score as follows:

10–14: If your answers are honest, you probably don't have a problem with feelings of pain and hurt.

15–22: You should give further consideration to the role of pain and hurt in your life.

23–30: You may be carrying a burden of emotional pain and hurt that you should come to terms with.

Your Feelings of Guilt

1. When things work in your favor, do you have a nagging sense that it shouldn't be happening?
2. Do you hold yourself back from taking steps that would change your life for the better?
3. Do you feel a sense of inner desperation?
4. Do you see your actions as threatening or damaging to yourself or others?
5. Do you have thoughts that you have harmed or disappointed people who are close to you?
6. Do you feel you don't deserve an intimate relationship with another person?
7. Do you do things that put your well-being in jeopardy?
8. Do you feel that you have things to atone for?

9. Are you troubled by a memory of how you said good-bye to someone who has died?
10. Do you have thoughts that you should have acted differently in some important situation?

Tally your points and evaluate your score as follows:

10–14: If your answers are honest, you probably don't have a problem with guilt.

15–22: You should give further consideration to the role of guilt in your life.

23–30: You may be carrying a burden of guilt that you should come to terms with.

CHAPTER 5

The Traps Your Hidden Feelings Create

The search for happiness is a curious thing. In our culture it is assumed that we all strive for the positive goals in life. We frequently tell ourselves and our neighbors about our quest for the good life and how much we deserve it. We cite years of struggle, of hard work, of doing for ourselves and our families as evidence that we are pursuing all the good that life has to offer.

Yet few people behave as though they truly believe they are entitled to happiness, success, and a satisfying life. The problem with the volumes of verbiage and thousands of magazine and television advertisements that claim to offer the key for happiness is that they ignore the darker side of the psyche—the hidden emotions that whisper or shout in our inner ear that we deserve nothing, that we should go to our graves miserable and alone. Our unresolved problems create obstacles to happiness.

"No matter what I do, I just can't seem to get hold of that wild blue yonder." This evocative statement, made by a man I treated in a drug-rehabilitation clinic, captures the sense of frustration we all feel at one time or another.

Bewilderment is a concomitant of the human condition. Many people go through life as sleepwalkers, confused, not knowing what is happening to them. Some of us are fortunate enough to go in and out of confusion and bewilderment. Others exist within it, accepting it as a state of being. The classic example is the person who's been in therapy for years standing at a cocktail party talking about his latest divorce and his fourth job in as many years.

In this chapter we will explore some of the traps our hidden emotions create. Spin-offs of anger, hurt, and guilt, these traps are a manifestation of our deepest feelings. Because they often serve as substitutes for the direct expression of those feelings, these traps also function as complex defenses.

Following each discussion is a set of questions by which you can test whether you have fallen into that trap. These quizzes are designed to improve your awareness of how you express your anger, hurt, and guilt.

The Trap of Self-Sabotage: The Agony of Success

Many of us do not like ourselves; in fact, many of us are filled with self-hate. We may feel we are not entitled to an intimate relationship with another person, to success at work, or to contentment with our lives in general.

On the surface we speak about wanting life's pleasures and rewards, but we may not be prepared to make them happen. We may keep ourselves away from people or from promising situations. We may be sarcastic and unpleasant or do things that work against our success, such as missing appointments, betraying confidences, drinking, gambling, or having affairs—whatever will put our well-being in jeopardy. Yet rare are those who are in touch with the fact that they dislike or hate themselves.

Self-hate sounds dramatic and extreme; it's not. Even though we might be unaware of them, most of us are capable of harboring intense negative feelings, even feelings of loathing, toward ourselves. The reason is that in many of our experiences with other people we see our behavior as appalling, disgraceful, or otherwise unacceptable. Unfortunately, we don't keep that feeling in focus long enough to truly face it and resolve it. Instead, it passes through our minds, a brief thought from which we quickly move away.

Some people who hate themselves have been "taught" to do so. In their earliest years, children often feel deeply hurt by the comparisons that their families make between them and siblings or other family members. Other people who do not like themselves suffer from guilt feelings, founded or unfounded, about relationships earlier in life. One person may feel he was unkind or ungrateful to his mother; another might be troubled by a memory of cruelly teasing his younger brothers.

Sometimes our guilt is too painful to face up to, and yet if we have a buried sense of guilt we live like the condemned anyway. People who feel guilty behave as though they must spend their lives atoning for some wrong they believe they have committed. Self-sabotage is the sentence they impose upon themselves, and often they try to make it into a life sentence. Even if they keep it below the level of their awareness, guilt brings with it a sense of uniqueness and the need to be secretly punished.

People who suffer from self-sabotage can be bewildered when other people leave or when they are rejected. They don't understand and often feel victimized. When they think about why things happen the way they do, they wonder about the wrong things. Usually the question should not be "Why did he go away?" but "What did I do to drive him away?" Instead of "Why did he decide to fire me?" they should ask "What did I do to cause him to fire me?" People have an easier time experiencing a sense of being victimized than guilt, which is the source of self-sabotage. They can explain in elaborate detail what was done to them, how they were cheated and abused. However, because of their difficulty in owning up to their self-centered impulses, they are mute when it comes to declaring what they did to others.

People sometimes sabotage themselves by focusing on guilt-provoking thoughts. One of my patients was tormented repeatedly by the idea that she would pick up a knife and murder her infant son. This pervasive thought caused her a great deal of anguish; in her mind it proved what a malignant creature she was. During her evaluation we learned that her experiences in childhood and early adulthood had created in her a severe sense of guilt that gave rise to an urge for self-sabotage. If it hadn't been for this woman's desire to punish herself, the murderous fantasy, when it first occurred, would have quickly dissipated and left her mind, but she had actively seized upon it as a weapon with which she could constantly punish herself. When she returned for her second session, she reported that she had felt some relief from the fantasy.

We must be vigilant about such thoughts, which, though they come into being as a self-punishing device, can take on a life of their own. Punishing thoughts can take any form: "I was not good to my mother before she died"; "I got a raise and my co-worker didn't, because I casually mentioned to a department manager that she had come in late"; "My neighbor got a new car, and I had a vision of it totally mangled in a car wreck; what a small-minded creature I am." These thoughts can range from petty notions to dramatic fantasies.

Self-sabotage can work in a variety of ways. Great suffering is frequently felt by people who experience a sense of lack of entitlement but succeed anyway, despite their best efforts to fail. I've had patients who hated themselves but by fluke succeeded—by virtue of a fruitful partnership, an idea whose time had come, or simply their excellent work—despite their self-loathing and guilt. However, their success simply reinforces their guilt and makes them more tense and unhappy.

Because on the surface their relationships and careers are positive and don't match the negative feelings and impulses that they harbor, these guilt-ridden people experience intense inner turmoil. Their urge to sabotage themselves and thus to assuage their guilt has been thwarted. What arises in its place is an inner sense of desperation. The need to explain this puzzling contradiction has given birth to such concepts as the midlife crisis and burnout.

Sometimes a person's sense of desperation is so great that he walks away from home and job and career, because he has no other way of punishing himself. He has failed at sabotaging his relationship or his work or his social life, so he drops out. If you ask him why, he offers philosophical reasons: "I need to find myself"; "I've got a good job and a wonderful family, but I've always been a malcontent"; "There's got to be more to life than this. I'm fifty years old. How much longer have I got?"

A sense of inner desperation is a signal that a person doesn't really like himself and thus can't tolerate success. Such people philosophize, intellectualize, and rationalize about where their unhappiness is coming from: "The world is not a nice place"; "There's so much injustice in life"; "What's the point of manufacturing widgets? Why aren't we selling heart-lung machines?" Because such defenses are laced with platitudes and valid concepts, the desperation is covered over. Yet the validity of the concepts does not erase the underlying negative emotions, nor does it mean that what someone is doing with his life is wrong.

If you have a sense of inner desperation and yet your life is satisfying in most other ways, or if you constantly sabotage your success, you may be suffering from self-hatred engendered by guilt.

Are You Trapped by Self-Sabotage?

In response to each question, rate yourself on a scale of 1 to 5:

1. Rarely or never
2. Sometimes
3. Often
4. Usually
5. Always

1. Do you have trouble understanding why bad things happen to you?
2. Do you think you've treated the people closest to you badly?
3. Do you deny yourself small pleasures when there's really no reason why you should?
4. Do you blame yourself when things go wrong?
5. Do you do things that appear foolish and then rationalize them away?
6. Do you pass up favorable opportunities without knowing why?
7. Do you spend more money than you should and get into debt?
8. Do you bicker with people around you?
9. Do you find yourself in a frenzy?
10. Do you question what you are doing with your life?

Add up your scores for all the questions and divide the total by 10. If your final score is 3 or higher, you may feel a need to punish yourself, to beat yourself up.

Fear of Your Own Anger

You've been looking forward to a meal at your favorite restaurant, but the roast beef is overcooked, the baked potato is cold, and you are irritated. Your dining partner says, "If you don't like your food, why don't you send it back?" But you don't, because you don't want to deal with the waiter.

Something similar can happen in relationships. When one person lets another down, the angry person often doesn't know how to deal with that emotion. He or she internalizes and seethes over it, and then does something else—usually something indirect—to ventilate the hostility. That indirect response could be to behave passively, to avoid contact, to show up late for appointments—any number of small, commonplace, irritating things. Or it could be an action that threatens the relationship.

Fear of your own anger may manifest itself as the inability to declare anger or negative feelings. Yet acknowledging anger is critically important. If you allow your defenses to shield you from feeling it, your anger is likely to dictate your attitudes and behavior. If you give in to a fear of your own anger, you may become a hostage to it.

Your anger may frighten you because earlier in life— say, in childhood—you had mixed feelings about someone close to you; you had the desire to be rid of that person or you wished that he or she would die. Because of that impulse, on one level you believe you have been "murderous." (This situation, of course, is intensified if anything does happen to that person.) You might also fear your anger because somewhere along the line you have experienced intense rage but suppressed it.

You might say, "I don't want to get angry because I'm afraid of what the other person might do to me in retaliation." You may really be anxious about what *you* might do if your own anger goes out of control. But you're not aware of that. You have rage impulses—perhaps homicidal fantasies—that you haven't come to grips with, and your fear is that if you give in to your anger, you'll lose control and hurt somebody.

If you have such perceptions—or misperceptions, since they're really only fantasies in most instances—you may have trained yourself not to show any anger at all because in your mind it's connected with potentially dangerous rage. When an experience early in life has been dramatic, the paralysis in terms of anger can be so great that you can be anxious about asserting yourself with a cashier who has given the wrong change.

This fear can be pervasive and can operate in the most mundane circumstances. It can also be severely incapacitating, as we saw in the case of Charles. Intelligent and well-educated, Charles was unsuccessful in most areas of his life. As we talked, he was at first unable to express any negative emotions. When he spoke about his unhappy childhood, I began to probe for how he had felt about his stepfather. His experiences in that relationship turned out to be the key to the paralysis that permeated his existence.

Charles's was burdened nearly to the point of emotional immobility by the intense anger that, as a teenager, he had felt against his abusive stepfather. Charles was so full of rage at this man that he had once come close to fulfilling his fantasy of wanting him dead, but he never faced that impulse until he came to therapy.

Charles's unacknowledged rage had resulted in guilt and self-sabotage. He rejected for no reason a scholarship to graduate school. Despite a college degree, he was employed in a menial job. In the course of his therapy, Charles moved away from the helpless position he had assumed to an awareness of some empathy for his stepfather and enormous pain at what he perceived the stepfather to be going through. He saw that his guilt had been masked by anger and how hurtful to him the conflict between his anger and his guilt was. His more balanced view of his relationship with his stepfather—in which he acknowledged affection as well as pain—was liberating.

Are You Trapped by Fear of Your Own Anger?

In response to each question, rate yourself on a scale of 1 to 5:

1. Rarely or never
2. Sometimes
3. Often
4. Usually
5. Always

1. When something annoys you, do you try to find a reason why it shouldn't?
2. When you get angry, are you the only one who knows it?
3. Are you troubled by memories of wanting someone to be out of your life?
4. In your mind, does anger mean going out of control?
5. When you feel angry, do you blame others?
6. Do you have fantasies about what you'd like to do to people who make you mad?
7. Do you hold your anger in check?
8. Do you feel you must protect other people from your anger?
9. Do you have fantasies of badly hurting or even killing people who make you angry?
10. In your mind, is anger a potentially overwhelming emotion?

Add up your scores for all the questions and divide the total by 10. If your final score is 3 or higher, you may be living in fear of your own anger.

The Victim Role

There can be a great allure in playing the role of a victim, in leading a life of imagined martyrdom.

Some people who take the position of victim act passive, deriving satisfaction from sympathy rather than from decisive action. Seeing that they can exert control over other people by appearing helpless, they try to make others feel guilty about their supposed victimization. Self-appointed victims use their helplessness to manipulate others. As they navigate obliquely through life, embracing the sense of being cheated, they learn that people respond to the mantle of victimization draped over their shoulders. Victims may not consciously say, "I'm going to relate to people in a passive way so as to manipulate them," but that's what they do, all the same.

Other victims take a more active stance, indulging in extended expressions of rage, either defensive anger or authentic anger that has been unduly prolonged. The anger we experience in our close relationships is almost always generated by what we perceive as rejection or abandonment. Such wounds to our self-image result in a deep sense of hurt, which then forms the foundation for anger. Being angry is a way of temporarily overcoming or trying to cover a profound sense of helplessness, powerlessness, inadequacy, or insignificance. When you become angry, you feel empowered by your rage. Throwing things around or having a tantrum gives you a momentary sense of power. But it's all compensatory and brings no resolution to the sense of hurt.

When this cycle of hurt and rage occurs frequently, especially in childhood, and when it concerns your parents or other key figures in your life, two things happen: the anger becomes habitual in an effort to cover the deepening sense of hurt, and the hurt becomes linked with a sense of inadequacy. You are conditioned through your experiences to believe you are insignificant and worthless. Your personality becomes centered around your experiences of rejection and infused with the anger with which you try to cover them. You develop an angry way of being that is based on feelings of worthlessness.

For angry victims, this ingrained rage can become exaggerated. If someone breaks into your car and steals your radio while you're at the movies, are you justified in being angry? Yes. What do you want to do about it? Do you want to go home, get a gun, and hunt for anybody who's breaking into cars? Probably not. Do you want to get an ulcer from it? No. Do you want to have repeated fantasies of catching that person and smashing him over the head with whatever is handy. That's one way of relieving yourself, but it's a masturbatory form of relief, with no reality to it.

Pain exists as part of the human condition. There is suffering in the world; there is injustice. People will treat you unfairly; fate will not be kind. Your decision-making process will not always be flawless and, perhaps more often than you want, may even undermine your goals. When bad things happen, you can feel persecuted, you can complain, you can lock yourself in the angry victim role—or you can acknowledge that this sort of thing is part of the human condition.

Because victimization is not something you can avoid, what you do about it is important. To pretend that something is an accident rather than a fact of life and a condition of existence is to misread things. Try to understand that you are very angry about what happened and spend your time productively taking steps to ensure that it won't happen again. Don't allow yourself to indulge in the role of victim and to remain enraged at the sense of having been cheated.

Are You Trapped in the Victim Role?

In response to each question, rate yourself on a scale of 1 to 5:

1. Rarely or never
2. Sometimes
3. Often
4. Usually
5. Always

1. Do you find it easier to be angry than to acknowledge feeling hurt?
2. Do you have angry fantasies?
3. Do you feel that you're not entitled to the good things in life?
4. Would you rather let other people make decisions?
5. When you feel angry, do you have a hard time calming down?
6. Do you believe that more bad than good has occurred in your life?
7. Do you find it difficult to get over bad experiences?
8. Do you have a hard time responding to or resolving situations that cause you emotional pain?
9. Do you have temper tantrums?
10. Do you feel inadequate?

Add up your scores for all the questions and divide the total by 10. If your final score is 3 or higher, you may see yourself as a victim.

The Fear of Closeness

You may claim that you want a love relationship, but underneath that expressed desire you may feel anxious about being close to someone.

Intimacy can be linked with emotional pain. Many people have had relationships early in life in which they were, or perceived themselves to be, disappointed, abandoned, or betrayed. If you are such a person, getting into a relationship may feel like running a risk. You may be afraid you'll experience more of the same.

Because death is ubiquitous, intimacy is frequently associated with emotions and memories of death. If your mother or father died or left the family during your childhood years, you may have felt great pain. You may be fearful that another close relationship will have a similar outcome. The association of intimacy with death can pervade the psyche. It's more than the thought, "I'm not going to get close to Alice, because I lost my mom when I was young. Mom's death hurt me terribly, and I don't want to get close to anyone else." It's deeper than that, a coloring of the emotions. The very idea of intimacy takes on a sad, depressive quality.

For people wounded by physical abuse, intimacy is connected with pain and fear. Emotional abuse is no less harmful. Many people grow up feeling that they are not good enough, that they can never achieve enough, no matter what they do. Therapists constantly hear "My father is never satisfied" or "My mother doesn't acknowledge my successes." Abuse also happens to adults, and it need not be as dramatic as wife-battering. If your partner constantly puts you down or is indifferent to you, it's hurtful.

People who harbor a fear of rejection have had emotionally traumatic experiences. Their anxiety is based on something real in their emotional past, usually a hurtful experience or a series of painful events. They have been unsuccessful in establishing relationships with someone they particularly desired, or their spouse or a lover may have had an affair with someone else. We speak of these people as having been "burned." They may show the world a face of cynicism or anger, but underneath there is a lot of pain.

People can also develop an aversion to closeness because of feelings of guilt: "I was not nice to my father before he died; therefore I don't deserve a relationship with another human being." These people are punishing themselves, telling themselves, "You've been a bad person in the past. Therefore you're no good. You're not entitled to close relationships."

To varying degrees, people affected by hurtful relationships suffer a sense of devaluation. Their estimation of who and what they are is diminished. They believe that they are not good enough and never will be good enough to accomplish their goals. Such self-devaluation is insidious and demoralizing.

Frequently we don't recognize how damaging these painful experiences can be because we are not aware of how extensively we have assimilated them into our personalities. In terms of intimate relationships, their major impact is on our ability to feel accepted, to feel a sense of worth, and to believe that we deserve the love and caring someone is attempting to give us. This inability in turn can affect our capacity to reciprocate those feelings; based on the pervasive sense of worthlessness that exists within us, we don't believe in our capacity to love and to care for another person.

Are You Trapped by a Fear of Closeness?

In response to each question, rate yourself on a scale of 1 to 5:

1. Rarely or never
2. Sometimes
3. Often
4. Usually
5. Always

1. Do you hesitate to confide your intimate thoughts and feelings to others?
2. Do you find yourself being critical of people who want to be close to you?
3. Do you associate closeness with painful or unhappy memories?
4. Do you have memories of being rejected or abandoned as a child by a parent or someone close to you?
5. Do movies about relationships make you sad?
6. Do you feel that your achievements never measure up to what other people accomplish?
7. Do you have difficulty accepting criticism from other people?
8. Have people close to you betrayed you?
9. Do memories of past relationships make you sad?
10. Do you feel you don't know how to care for another person?

Add up your scores for all the questions and divide the total by 10. If your final score is 3 or higher, you may be suffering from a fear of closeness.

Sexual Problems

Your defenses and your most painful hidden emotions can act to the detriment of the sexual part of a relationship. Sexual behavior does not exist solely in and of itself, unrelated to the other areas of your life. Everything that you find sexually stimulating or inhibiting is linked with another issue in your past or present.

Sexual Prohibitions, Inhibitions, and Guilt

Many people tell me, "As I grew up, we never discussed sex in our household." In many families, sex is something that is done only for "appropriate" reasons and only under "appropriate" circumstances. It's very easy to move from the notion of "appropriate" sex to the notion that sex should make you feel guilty. The ways the people around us have behaved sexually or their attitudes about sex—and the results— can have a strong impact on an experience that should be pleasurable and satisfying.

Prohibitions and inhibitions, which can be complex and elaborate, are often based on earlier experiences. Sexual abuse of children is one fertile source. Another is behavior on the part of a parent. For instance, the behavior of a promiscuous parent or one who leaves the home for another relationship can have a major impact on a child's attitudes toward sex. The children of such parents may view sex as a dangerous force that can threaten a family's foundations; as a result, these children may try hard to be stable and to control their sexual urges.

Having a prohibition or an inhibition about sex is in itself not a bad thing. It becomes a problem when your partner does not share it. Such a situation can result in a contest of wills, bruised egos, and hurt feelings.

Fear of Sexual Fantasies

Because they're not understood, sexual fantasies can sometimes be threatening. Fantasizing about a kind of sexual activity that isn't practiced in a relationship can be anxiety-provoking because of prohibitions. For example, within a heterosexual relationship, homoerotic fantasies can be very anxiety-provoking. When someone has a fantasy that is homoerotic in nature, the immediate response is "I must be homosexual," and most people react with consternation to that possibility.

Homoerotic fantasies are commonly born of a craving for closeness with the parent of the same sex. Frequently people perceive their relationship with that parent as difficult or distant or cold or not the way they want it to be, and a homoerotic fantasy represents the desire for attention and warmth. Most people's homoerotic fantasies mainly involve fondling, touching, and holding.

Sexual fantasies represent a need—one that can emanate from the distant past, the recent past, or the present. The thing to keep in mind is that the fantasy can be understood. When you are concerned about how terrible a fantasy is, you should ask yourself how much of your concern is self-sabotage—the desire to not enjoy sex or to put a wall between yourself and your partner.

Confusing Tender Feelings with Sexual Feelings

I often see cases in which people define themselves through their sexuality; in other words, they feel that if they're not perceived as sexual beings, then there's something wrong with them—they've failed. Such people tend to confuse tender feelings with sexual feelings.

A man named Jason came to me agonizing about getting a divorce. He was having great difficulty with the thought of leaving his wife and children, an action he contemplated because he was involved in a sexual relationship with Nancy, a woman he worked with. Jason described their relationship as a working friendship that, over a period of months, had evolved into an affair as they traveled together on company business. Jason reported that Nancy also was suffering with the idea of divorcing her husband. Both felt tremendous guilt about the prospect of leaving their spouses, and neither identified major problems in their marriages.

It became clear during the evaluation session that Jason had misconstrued his feelings about Nancy. According to him, they had not felt physically attracted to each other initially. Nancy had always been considerate of his needs and feelings as they worked together, and she often helped him and made his life easier. As Jason described his very warm, tender feelings about her, it became clear to him that he had confused these tender feelings with sexual feelings.

Jason came to understand that, while he cared for Nancy very much, this caring was different from the love one feels for someone with whom one wants to share a lifetime. Over the next few weeks, he had conversations with Nancy. She expressed a sense of relief, admitting that she, too, had entered the sexual relationship because of tender feelings toward him.

In the course of therapy, Jason was able to relate sexual impulses toward women who were kind to him to several significant relationships in his life. Jason and Nancy continued to be very close friends, but their physical relationship ended. On follow-up, Jason reported that his marriage continued to be a good one. As an aside, he stated that Nancy also continued to be happily married.

You may confuse tender feelings with sexual feelings when someone treats you well and when you don't have faith in yourself. You don't like yourself and don't believe that your friendship is enough. The only thing you know how to give is your sexuality.

When you get into a relationship, not only do you confuse tender feelings with sexual feelings; you then confuse sexual feelings with love. You might even end your marriage, but in two or three months your relationship with your new lover may end because it wasn't based on a deep sense of caring.

Lack of Honesty about Sex

Lack of sexual honesty means not being open about sexual things that you find pleasurable or exciting, or not facing your anxiety about sex.

Sexual honesty is very important when one partner has desires or inhibitions that the other does not share. These issues have to be talked out. If they're not, the result will be such defenses as avoidance, rationalization, and anger, beneath them, the clash will continue to threaten the relationship.

Sex affects and makes a statement about many other key issues in our lives: our self-esteem, our self-worth, our sense of effectiveness. A poor sexual relationship can affect the other areas of our existence because it undermines how we think about ourselves. Sexual fears and anxieties can lead to a perception of sexual and even personal failure, in what can be a cumulative process of demoralization.

If you do not deal with your sexual problems, your self-worth may be put in question and your fear of rejection may be heightened. If you and your partner ignore the existence of a problem, sex may become a perfunctory activity that takes place infrequently. Instead of talking about it, you may treat it like a skeleton in the closet. Dismissing sex as unimportant is one of the most significant components in the creation of a dysfunctional relationship and can even lead to the demise of a relationship.

When you and your partner do not discuss sex openly, you exacerbate two dangerous situations: you don't allow for intimacy, and you encourage misperceptions, anxieties, guilt, and inhibitions. Then you blame each other and at the same time blame yourselves. This is an unwholesome background for a mutually sustaining relationship. If the lack of self-esteem is very intense, frequently one or both of you may look to someone else for support and sexual attention.

Are You Trapped by Sexual Problems?

In response to each question, rate yourself on a scale of 1 to 5:

1. Rarely or never
2. Sometimes
3. Often
4. Usually
5. Always

1. Does sex make you feel guilty?
2. Do you see sex as something threatening?
3. Do you feel sexually inept?
4. Do your sexual fantasies frighten you?
5. Does the idea of a satisfying sex life make you uneasy?
6. Do you hesitate to speak frankly with your partner about sexual matters?
7. Do you and your partner have significantly different ideas about sex?
8. Do you feel sexually misunderstood?
9. Do you have memories in which sex has an unpleasant or frightening connotation?
10. Do you frequently eroticize relationships with acquaintances and co-workers?

Add up your scores for all the questions and divide the total by 10. If your final score is 3 or higher, your defenses and deep, hidden emotions may be manifesting themselves in your sex life.

Ambivalence—Living in a Neutral Zone

In one form or another, the ambivalent person repeats the statement: "I don't know what I want." Ambivalence can be the product of guilt, anger, or pain; it is a state of mind perpetuated by chronic defensiveness. An ambivalent position is an implicit decision to remain trapped by inaction. It's what you're stuck in when you haven't decided to give up your defenses and make a success of your life.

By definition, ambivalence involves mixed feelings. There may be an impulse to move in one direction, but another impulse counterbalances it. For example, a patient of mine was ambivalent about leaving a job in which he was miserable because he had a difficult boss. On another level, however, this man reminded him in a negative way of his father; staying in the job allowed him to replay the guilt he felt for distancing himself from his father and to punish himself in the process.

Ambivalence can enhance your view of yourself as a victim, because if you're not going to take charge, there's always someone around who will. Passivity and a willingness to be manipulated promote a heightened sense of victimization, which can lead to a nonproductive and depleting cycle of hurt and anger. By utilizing defenses and locking yourself into a position of ambivalence, you manage to maintain the status quo. It's a perfect way to quietly sabotage yourself.

You're making plans for the evening and your friend says, "Where do you want to eat?" You say, "I don't care." Now, you may not have a strong preference, but if you're really honest with yourself, you know what you want that night. You know that you'd like pasta rather than Japanese food. You have a point of view, but for whatever reason you edit yourself and come out with an ambivalent statement. We also do this in more complicated areas of our lives, such as work.

Ambivalent people constantly censor their conversation. They abbreviate or alter information in order to avoid facing the emotions and impulses that they fear. For example, you may not want to upset your parents by saying, "I've been offered a great job out of town and I'm going to take it." Because of practical problems that would have to be faced, in your mind the difficult issues loom large and the rewards and pleasures shrink. Because of your anxieties or your sense of lack of entitlement, you eliminate various components of the decision and turn down the offer.

The right decision is usually clear. Telling yourself you don't know what to do is a subterfuge that serves only to maintain the status quo. In fact you do know.

Should you take that job in another city? Most of the time you know how you feel in your present position and what its potential is. You are able to assess the myriad issues that affect you: your relationship with your co-workers, how you're viewed in the company, your relationship with your superiors, the limitations of the new company, all the pros and cons. If you force yourself to be honest, in most cases you know what you need to do.

Rather than calling up on their mental computer screen all the information they have, ambivalent people just punch in a few pieces of data that will serve to sustain the status quo. Even when they look for advice, they seek only the counsel that they want to hear.

In making decisions, most people do not need to consult a third party, except sometimes for technical expertise. Your own decision-making ability is usually sufficient, because you know the nuances of the situation and—most important—of your own inner feelings. When you censor yourself you get a watered-down version of that knowledge, a version that serves your fears and anxieties.

You are the world's leading authority on your feelings, and yet you can use your defenses to keep from being in touch with those feelings. You can take an inventory of the pros and cons of a situation and make an assessment of it but *choose* not to. You may even take the ambivalent position willfully and then rationalize why you've taken it.

You need to take charge of your life. Do you want to censor yourself and stay in an emotional neutral zone or do you want to take action?

Are You Trapped by Ambivalence?

In response to each question, rate yourself on a scale of 1 to 5:

1. Rarely or never
2. Sometimes
3. Often
4. Usually
5. Always

1. Do you feel that you are going in circles?
2. Do you make excuses when things don't work out for you?
3. Do you settle for second best in your work and relationships?
4. Do you find it difficult to state your preferences?
5. Do you stay in unpleasant situations without knowing why?
6. Is the unknown intimidating to you?
7. Do you leave decisions to other people?
8. Do you anguish over decisions that other people seem to make easily?
9. Do you tend to play it safe?
10. Do your decisions result in a maintenance of the status quo?

Add up your scores for all the questions and divide the total by 10. If your final score is 3 or higher, you may be someone who avoids taking action and moving forward.

Isolation: The Separation of Thought and Feeling

People use the defense of avoidance to stay away from interactions with others that might involve painful or unpleasant feelings. Isolated people avoid any connections with their emotions. They "split off," or separate, their thoughts and experiences from the emotions connected with them. Some people can become so isolated that their thoughts and emotions no longer coincide and there's an internal disassociation of feeling and intellect.

Sometimes the isolation of thought from feeling is a result of the defense of intellectualization ("That's the way life is") or helplessness ("I don't know what you mean"). Rationalization can also be called up in the service of isolation ("I understand why he got so upset with me. He's under a lot of stress"), as can denial ("I don't feel sad; I don't feel anything"). Isolation is frequently experienced by people who have feelings of guilt.

If you have difficulty answering the question "What is a feeling?" you may suffer from an isolation of thought from emotion. The challenge is to bring the two into sync so that when you have an experience, you recognize the emotion that goes with it. When that doesn't happen, you live within a walled city and intimacy is very difficult to accomplish.

At the beginning of the evaluation session with Charles in Chapter 1, the schism within his personality between thought and feeling was obvious. Only after I repeatedly challenged his defenses of vagueness, rationalization, and intellectualization did he become aware of the emotions he was harboring.

Emotionally isolated people are often perceived as cold and aloof. A daughter might view her father as someone who doesn't have a lot to give, when the father is really a person who suffers from the isolation of thought from feeling; the emotions are there, but they are blocked. They are not integrated with the man's other mental processes.

How does someone come to suffer this isolation of thought from feeling? Through a persistent use of the defenses, which serve to block out the feelings. There is a direct correlation between the use of defenses and the degree of isolation a person experiences. Some people use certain defenses infrequently, and other people employ them as a way of life, but everyone has used all of them at some time.

The very defended person is a very isolated person. The slightly defended person is minimally isolated. But because we all use defenses, every one of us suffers from some degree of isolation. It's a fact of existence. One goal of any corrective emotional experience is to minimize that isolation, to allow thought and emotion to coexist, and to permit ourselves to enjoy a sense of accomplishment and satisfaction in life.

Breaking through our defenses puts us face to face with the emotional issues that trouble us the most. Grappling with those issues and working them through to resolution means seeing our problems in perspective and coming to a balanced view of our relationships with others. Intimacy is an invaluable asset and a key element in this process of emotional change.

But isolation precludes intimacy. Extremely isolated people—those who refuse to bring their emotions into their awareness—cannot be intimate. Conversely, intimate people are not isolated, either from their own deepest feelings or from other people.

Are You Trapped by Isolation?

In response to each question, rate yourself on a scale of 1 to 5:

1. Rarely or never
2. Sometimes
3. Often
4. Usually
5. Always

1. Do you have difficulty talking about your emotions?
2. Do you sense a distance between yourself and the events that take place around you?
3. Do you keep your feelings under control?
4. Do you use your mind more than your emotions?
5. Do you feel puzzled when other people get upset about things?
6. Do you feel that you "stay on the surface" in your conversations with people?
7. Is it easy for you to explain the actions of someone who lets you down?
8. Does the idea of confiding your personal feelings to another person make you nervous?
9. Do you feel that life is filled with problems and that there is nothing to be gained from getting upset about them?
10. Do you often have trouble explaining how you feel?

Add up your scores for all the questions and divide the total by 10. If your final score is 3 or higher, an isolation of thought from feeling may be blocking your sense of satisfaction and well-being.

PART II

The Defenses in Action: Understanding and Moving Past Them

I n chapters 6, 7, and 8, I will present several case studies from actual therapy sessions. I hope that reading about how the defenses operated in the lives of these people—and how discarding their emotional smoke screens let them work through their greatest emotional difficulties— will help you see how your own defenses interfere in your life and how you can benefit from breaking free of them.

First, take the following simple quiz, designed to show you which defenses you use the most. All you have to do is choose the statements you would be likely to make. Don't take too much time to think about each one. When a statement rings true as something you might say or agree with, jot down the number, and move on to the next one.

After you've reviewed all the statements, turn to the end of the quiz for a key to the defenses these statements reflect. Two or three will probably emerge as your favorite defenses.

1. I haven't done anything all day, but I'm just too tired to go to the party.
2. I can't go to the party—I don't have a date!
3. When my boyfriend told me I should consider going on a diet, I really gave him a piece of my mind.
4. My cousin and I had a silly argument. We sort of made up, but I guess I'm still a little mad at her.
5. What is life all about anyway?
6. I want a better job, but I don't know what to do about it.
7. I haven't had much interest in sex recently.
8. I didn't mean to forget my mother's birthday—it's just that I've been so busy at work.
9. Most nights I go to bed earlier than my husband.
10. What can you expect from people? They're bound to disappoint you.
11. My husband gets angry a lot, but I try to be nice so he'll calm down.
12. I don't know why—I just feel blue.
13. My blind date was interesting, but I had a big project due at work, so I never called him again.
14. My wife has been drinking a lot again, and then my son came home with two D's on his report card. I really gave it to that kid!
15. When my mother lays her guilt trips on me, sometimes I feel kind of frustrated.
16. Life is a constant battle.
17. I want to find someone to have a relationship with, but I can't stand the dating scene.
18. Sure it takes a lot of time and my wife and kids do complain, but I love working on my hobby.
19. My wife is just like her mother!
20. When my boyfriend said he thought we should see other people, it made me feel kind of uneasy.
21. My wife usually decides where we'll go on vacation.
22. My best friend says I've put on some weight, but personally I don't see it.

23. Mostly I just page through the newspaper and look at the ads. I can't concentrate on the articles.
24. All my friends are married—how can I expect to meet anyone?
25. My best friend is the one who really understands me. When my wife and I have a problem, I always go talk it out with him.
26. We were supposed to visit my in-laws on Saturday, but my son forgot to clean out the garage and that got me so irritated I stayed home.
27. I like to go with the flow.
28. They don't know what they're talking about.
29. What I like to do on dates is go to the movies.
30. My boss yelled at me again yesterday. I guess I'd better think about getting my act together.
31. C'est la vie!
32. My boss constantly tells me I'm disorganized and unfocused, but I do as well as the next person.
33. Other people seem to have such good ideas about interesting things to do, but I'm in a rut.
34. Why should I share my opinions with my boss? She never listens to me anyway.
35. Being with my family is too stressful for me. I see them about once a year.
36. I don't know why I didn't get that promotion last year. I've felt sort of upset ever since.
37. If you're human, you suffer. That's the way it is.
38. My brother says that I come across as angry a lot of the time, but I don't agree. I'm not like that.
39. I have this pain. I can't really describe it, but it worries me. What if I have a serious disease?
40. When I get angry, it's best for me to get out of the house.
41. When things don't go right for me on a job, I tell the boss off and quit.
42. I'm not sure, but I think I might be depressed.

43. Men and women just don't understand one another. It's a law of nature.
44. When it comes to deciding where to go, I usually leave it up to my date.
45. My brother claims he has evidence that Dad is having an affair, but I'm sure it's not true.
46. I didn't do much on the weekend—just stayed in bed.
47. I have a lot of special qualities, but most people don't appreciate them.
48. When my husband forgot our anniversary, I blew up at him!
49. Life has a lot of pain and hurt in store for most people.
50. I can't stand confrontation.
51. Okay, I'm spending more than I'm earning, but something will happen and things will turn out fine.
52. When my wife is grouchy, I stay out of her way.
53. When my date didn't like the casserole I cooked for dinner, I got so annoyed that I refused to go to the movies.
54. Sometimes when I think about how the new kid in the next office gets all the good projects, I feel kind of down.
55. I think it's best to be agreeable when it's at all possible.
56. My doctor says I have high blood pressure, but that's impossible. I feel just fine.

Key to the Quiz

Check the list below for the defenses reflected by the statements you chose. You'll probably find that you use two or three defenses more than others.

1. depression	5. intellectualization	9. avoidance
2. rationalization	6. helplessness	10. intellectualization
3. anger	7. depression	11. helplessness
4. vagueness	8. rationalization	12. depression

13. rationalization   28. denial   43. intellectualization
14. anger   29. avoidance   44. helplessness
15. vagueness   30. vagueness   45. denial
16. intellectualization 31. intellectualization 46. depression
17. rationalization   32. denial   47. rationalization
18. avoidance   33. depression   48. anger
19. anger   34. rationalization 49. intellectualization
20. vagueness   35. avoidance   50. helplessness
21. helplessness   36. vagueness   51. denial
22. denial   37. intellectualization 52. avoidance
23. depression   38. denial   53. anger
24. rationalization   39. depression   54. vagueness
25. avoidance   40. avoidance   55. helplessness
26. anger   41. anger   56. denial
27. helplessness   42. vagueness

The three chapters that follow describe problems some of my patients have had in relationships, in work situations, and when faced with a loss. These case studies and the self-exploration that ends Chapter 8 will help you to recognize and understand the defenses and to see how they stand in your way as you seek a more satisfying life.

CHAPTER 6

The Masks We Wear in Relationships

Perceptions of relationships are like the attempts of the blind men who described an elephant. One felt the tail and said the elephant was long and thin, like a snake. Another laid his hand on the leg and claimed the elephant was shaped like a tree trunk. Another felt the tusk and envisioned a beast covered with a heavy shell. From their limited perspectives, each provided a drastically different description. The same thing happens as we perceive our relationships.

Frequently the way you view your relationships is molded by painful emotions and impulses that emanate from other areas of your life, past and present, and that have little to do with the relationship itself. The masks you wear—the defenses you use in a vain effort to protect yourself from your emotions and impulses—can further obscure your view of another person and of your relationship. And when you wear masks, the face you put forward to the other person is not the true you.

The role of your defenses is complicated and exaggerated by the defenses and behaviors of the other person. When your distorted view of relating interacts with your partner's distorted view, the result is a relationship that's misperceived by both of you. Nevertheless, that's the relationship you both respond to.

The defenses mire us down in emotional patterns that block our ability to be intimate, to be in the moment, and to perceive the elements of a relationship in a way that is productive. If we can take off our masks—get rid of our defenses—we can more accurately perceive what our closest relationships are really about.

Intimacy with another person is not a natural instinct. Rather it is an ability that we must learn and that we must constantly strive to maintain. A deep, underlying problem may be preventing you from finding and keeping a satisfying relationship. Breaking through your defenses and working through your most painful problems will make you better able to get on with the pleasure, enjoyment, and satisfaction that a truly close personal relationship can bring.

Here are some conversations with patients of mine who misperceived their relationships.

A Movie Review

John and his wife, Alice, had just seen the classic movie *Anna Karenina*.

Alice: Wow, was that a great movie!
John: It was all right.
Alice: Garbo was terrific in that part. When she left her husband to be with someone she really loved—I think that took courage. Not every woman could do that.
John: I thought it was stupid. It wasn't realistic.
Alice: Of course it was realistic!
John: What was she going to do for the rest of her life?

It'll be very exciting when she's living in a cold-water flat and can't afford groceries.

Alice: There are more important things in life than money.

John: Here we go again. Like what?

Alice: It's impossible to discuss anything with you.

John: What is there to discuss? It isn't fun being Anna Karenina in real life. This idiot turns her back on her responsibilities and runs off into the sunset. To you, that's romantic. If you ask me, she *should* have been hit by a train.

Alice: You take the fun out of everything. What are you getting so angry about? It was only a movie.

Something was going on in this conversational Tower of Babel, but what? When I focused on John's defenses, his real feelings came out.

Zois: How did you feel when she said it was a great movie?

John: Well, you know, she always goes overboard.

Zois: But what was your emotion?

John: I guess I was angry. [vagueness]

Zois: You say "I guess."

John: I was angry. [anger]

Zois: What comes to your mind?

John: I just don't know what to do to make her see that we have a good life together. [helplessness]

Zois: So you see yourself as the victim who's carrying the relationship.

John: Well, whenever we have one of these discussions, I get angry; then she gets superior and makes me feel like an idiot. The next couple of days are ruined for me. I can't get our quarrel out of my head. I just lie around mulling over what she said and what I said, and I can't get interested in anything else. [depression]

Zois: You see yourself as crippled.

John: What do you mean?

Zois: How do you feel when you ask me the question "What do you mean?"

John: I don't know where you get these ideas. It annoys me. You constantly say things like that to me.

Zois: You don't want me to see past the victim position that you assume.

With minimal pressure and challenge to his defenses, John was able to acknowledge his emotions. Because his cognitive process and his emotions were not very much out of sync, I was able to guide his thoughts and feelings onto the same track. He quickly came to see where his defenses placed him—in the angry victim role. I was then able to help him make the transition to the tender, feeling side of his psyche.

Nevertheless, John manifested the irritation and anger that all of us feel when our defenses are challenged. Likewise, when you look at your behavior, you may find it difficult to scrutinize your problems. It is helpful to keep in mind that, to a greater or lesser degree, you are going to resist admitting to yourself things that you don't like about yourself.

John acknowledged his anger, including his anger at me for pointing out that he used his passivity in an aggressive way and that he wrapped himself in the mantle of the victim as a way to express hostility and anger toward his wife. He was then able to come to terms with his underlying anxiety that he was not "in control" of their relationship and that his wife would be unfaithful to him. It was this anxiety that made him provoke their quarrels. Now when she behaves independently or admires someone else's independence, he can discuss his feelings with her in more realistic terms; he has allowed himself to become closer to her.

When people speak of having problems with control or of being a "control freak," what they are usually saying is that their behavior is not eliciting the desired result from another person. In effect, they are putting their well-being into the hands of another. Instead of being dependent on someone else's attitudes and behavior, your goal should be to make statements or to act on your own behalf. If the response you receive is satisfying, that's all to the good, but you should not perceive it as essential to your well-being. If you can let go of the need to get the desired result from somebody else—the need to be an emotional hostage to that person—you will have let go of the need to "control."

A Broken Date

All week Sheila had been looking forward to spending Saturday evening with her boyfriend, Peter. As he had done in the past, Peter called at the last minute:

Peter: I can't make it tonight. I have to work late.
Sheila: I don't believe it! [anger] I changed other plans in order to see you. [victimization]
Peter: I'm sorry, Sheila, but I have a report to finish.
Sheila: Now what am I going to do? You always do this to me. [helplessness]
Peter: I said I can't make it. What do you want from me anyway?
Sheila: What should I want? I can't believe I'm involved with you. You're the most inconsiderate person I know. (She slams down the phone.)

As Sheila and I talked during her next therapy session, it became clear that she had responded with rage and helplessness, plus a bit of the victim role, as a cover for her hurt feelings at being rejected.

Sheila: I can't stand him. I really hate him. [anger]
Zois: As you say that, you appear tearful. Are you?
Sheila: Yes.
Zois: Are you holding the tears back?

Sheila: Yes.
Zois: You don't want me to see your feelings. You want to keep me at a distance. You don't want me to be useful to you.

I focused on Sheila's attempt to distance herself from me—essentially a defensive maneuver. Dealing with it smoothed the way for me to elicit the painful emotions she was trying to hide.

Zois: What is the emotion that you are hiding under that anger, that you don't want me to see?
Sheila: I feel so hurt. (She starts to cry.)
Zois: So your anger covers a great deal of pain.
Sheila: I hate to feel this way.
Zois: It's difficult to acknowledge how you suffer with these painful feelings.

Sheila was using anger to defend against hurt. For her this broken date was not a simple interaction with someone who had work to do and couldn't see her; she perceived herself as being rejected and therefore felt devalued.

Only when she was able to put aside her rage and her sense of being a victim could Sheila admit to herself how painful Peter's rejection was. She was able to experience the hurt and to connect it with her realization that she had allowed a deep sadness to control her life; she saw that each time someone let her down her sadness became more acute.

Past and present experiences determine how we behave in relationships. At another point in her therapy, Sheila had talked about her mother. When I heard how Sheila responded to her, I felt I had come upon the training ground where Sheila had first learned how to deal—that is, *not* deal—with hurt feelings.

Sheila told me about a phone conversation with her mother.

Mother: I tried to call you this morning before work, but as usual you weren't home.

Sheila: Oh.

Mother: I wanted to remind you to send Aunt Cynthia a get-well card. You know how much she cares about you.

Sheila: Of course I will. I'm glad you called. I was wondering if I could bring Peter home for dinner Sunday. I'd like you to meet him.

Mother: Not this Sunday, dear. I don't want to worry you, but I haven't been feeling well. Having company for dinner would just be too much for me.

Sheila: Mom, would you please go to the doctor? You never take care of yourself. You know I worry about you. And it's okay about dinner. Maybe I can bring him another time.

Mother: Don't worry about me. I'll just make do the best I can. You have your own life to lead.

As Sheila and I reviewed the phone call, I focused on her defense of helplessness.

Zois: When your mother said you weren't in when she called, what did you say?

Sheila: Well, basically, I said nothing. I just said "Oh." [helplessness]

Zois: How did you feel as you said "Oh"?

Sheila: She makes me feel so guilty, and I never know what to say to her.

Zois: What else did you feel?

Sheila: I guess I was angry.

Zois: You say you guess.

Sheila: I was angry.

Zois: What comes to your mind?

Sheila: She is so judgmental.

Zois: What did you want to say to your mother when she asked you that question?
Sheila: I would like to have said, "I was with my boyfriend that night."

In simply replying "Oh," Sheila alerted her mother that she was feeling guilty and helpless, that she was not prepared to challenge her mother's control or stand up to her anger. In a sense, through her defensiveness she authored her mother's response. She stood before her as a naughty little girl who was hiding something, rather than as a self-sufficient adult who could make her own decisions. Her mother's judgment hurt Sheila; it meant that, although she was an adult, she couldn't be open with her mother about an important relationship in her life.

As she did with Peter, Sheila learned to see how she used defenses to deal with the emotions elicited by her relationship with her mother. Once she faced the feelings of hurt that she had buried, she stopped covertly giving her mother permission to be judgmental and disapproving.

Sheila had accepted her mother's point of view and made it her own. She was dimly aware that this had happened but didn't understand it with clarity. She was unable to say, "Mother, you make me feel bad about myself," but she felt the hurt and remained vulnerable to her mother's statements. Once Sheila took inventory of the chain of emotions generated in her interactions with her mother, she was able to identify the part of her that believed the message; she was able to clarify it and free herself of it.

In the past, when Peter or someone else "rejected" Sheila—behaved toward her in a way that replicated the negative judgment of her mother—she had responded with exaggerated hurt and pain, because she wasn't responding only to Peter; she was also responding to her mother, the significant figure who stood behind him. Putting her emotions about her mother in balance helped to defuse the hurt and pain she felt when someone broke a date or let her down in some other way. She still felt some hurt and some irritation, but it wasn't so exaggerated as it had been in the past; it became manageable. Sheila began to deal appropriately with relationships and not to take a victim role as a way of avoiding the complex feelings that were tugging at her. She no longer found herself locked in rage and frustration, struggling to control pent-up feelings of pain and hurt.

By demonstrating that she could withstand disapproval and that she had faith in a value system of her own, Sheila showed her mother that her disapproval would no longer work as a means to inspire guilt and exert control. Her mother accommodated Sheila's new outlook. They built a new relationship based on mutual respect rather than on passivity and intimidation.

When one person in a relationship modifies his attitude and behavior, sometimes the other person notices that she is not getting the usual response and, as a result, changes her own behavior. This may not happen in every instance, but it's something to consider when you're questioning why you should go to the trouble of making a statement on your own behalf. You're making the statement for yourself; you should not expect to alter the attitudes and behavior of another person. But sometimes such a change does occur.

A Crisis

Richard, a man in his thirties, complained of being depressed. His relationship with his wife was very strained. He perceived her as constantly picking on him and harassing him, and he identified his depression as the result of the marital problems.

During the evaluation session, it became clear that Richard was contributing to his wife's anger by his own angry behavior and attitudes, which extended into their sex life. He expressed his anger toward his wife by avoiding her sexually. He went to bed late, when she was already asleep. He got up earlier than she did. Because they didn't discuss sex, he never had to give a reason for avoiding her, but circumstances resulted in a lack of physical warmth and exchange, sexual or otherwise, for weeks at a time.

Avoidance was the way Richard dealt with all the significant people in his life when he faced problems and conflicts with them. The same had been true of his father, who had died when Richard was in his early teens; he remembered their unresolved relationship as characterized by a lack of communication. And he had behaved the same way with his brother.

Zois: You discussed with me your anger with your wife and your anger with me. Is there anyone else who makes you angry?

Richard: You mean now?

Zois: Any time.

Richard: No. [denial]

Zois: You say no.

Richard: That's right.

Zois: So, over the years, the only two people who have made you angry are your wife and me.

Richard: (Pauses) Yes.

When I saw how committed Richard was to the defense of denial, I realized that he was harboring significant anger. Obviously no one goes through life feeling angry only with his wife and his therapist. I pressed the point.

Zois: There was no one else? Are you censoring yourself?

Richard: Well, maybe my brother. [vagueness]

Zois: You say "maybe" your brother.

Richard: Yes, my brother.

Zois: What are your thoughts?

Richard: That he hasn't been a very good brother, and
I'm angry with him.

Zois: What comes to your mind?

Richard: He hasn't been good to me throughout my life.

Zois: What's your relationship with your brother like
now?

Richard: He's terminally ill.

Richard had mixed feelings about his brother, which
included superficial anger. He was not in touch with his
tender feelings; instead he was in the angry victim mode.
Richard's anger at his brother was unacceptable because of
his brother's imminent death; therefore he displaced it onto
his wife to a greater degree than he had in the past. In
other words, the crisis about his brother's death caused him
to channel more of his negative emotions to his wife than he
had before.

Zois: What was your relationship with your brother
when you were growing up?

Richard: It was never good, and after my father died it
got worse. It was just me and my brother and
my mother living at home, and he was her favorite.
He used to always pick on me.

Zois: What are the positive things that you remember
about your brother?

Richard: None. [denial]

Zois: You say none. How old are you now?

Richard: Thirty-four.

Zois: So in thirty-four years you can't remember one
positive thing about your brother.

Richard: Well, there was one time he took me to a basketball
game soon after my father died. He was four years
older than me. I was fourteen and he was eighteen.
He bought me a hot dog and a soda, and we
really had a good time talking about the game.

Zois: So there are positive memories.
Richard: It was only that one time.
Zois: You want to minimize it.

I tried to move Richard from the position of angry victim to an acknowledgment of the good feelings that exist in every relationship. He was so deeply committed to his anger that at first I got him to grudgingly admit only one. Later in the interview he described other feelings, which culminated in the following interchange.

Zois: How do you feel now as you think about your brother dying?
Richard: I feel very sad.
Zois: What would you miss about him?
Richard: Some of those good times that we talked about before.
Zois: When did you have those thoughts about the good times?
Richard: Here, today, for the first time in all these years.

What Richard said validates the theory that if the therapist stays with the defenses and exhausts them, he will be rewarded with a rich amount of significant emotional material. At this stage, I had helped Richard begin to move from anger to the tender feelings that would allow him to have a balanced view of his relationship with his brother and that would help diminish the guilt we would discuss in subsequent sessions. As his guilt abated, his ability to be intimate with his brother increased. I used this same technique as we considered Richard's relationship with his wife, his father, his mother, and myself.

Immediately after the above exchange, Richard talked about his guilt and tearfully described his painful feelings about his brother.

Zois: You say your brother is dying.

Richard: Yes.

Zois: And we see you have a lot of feelings about that. Have you declared your positive feelings to your brother?

Richard: No.

Zois: What are your thoughts about that?

Richard: I've been unable to do that. [helplessness]

Zois: So you're taking a helpless position.

Richard: Well, I know I should do it.

Zois: You say you know you should, but what are you going to do about it?

Richard: I guess I should go see him. [vagueness]

Zois: You say you guess. As with other issues in your life, you're again sitting on the fence. You want to put yourself in a situation where he'll die and you'll be left with all these feelings unresolved, not having declared your emotions. So why do you want to do this to yourself?

Richard: It's not a good feeling.

Zois: Have you behaved this way with anybody else?

Richard: Yes.

Zois: With who?

Richard: My wife.

Zois: What comes to your mind?

Richard: In the same way I was angry with my brother I am angry with her, and I see from our discussion today that a lot of that anger is not merited.

At this point we examined parallels between Richard's behavior toward his brother and his behavior toward his wife. We then linked that behavior to his perceived relationship with his father and to his attempt to keep a wall between himself and me. An important aspect of the short-term technique is to connect patients' feelings about people from their current life, people from their past, and the therapist. An awareness of these connections makes it easier for patients to identify patterns of feeling, and it combats the tendency to view their emotions toward any one person as singular and unique.

Although he wasn't at first aware of it, Richard had entered therapy in a crisis stimulated by the diagnosis of his brother's terminal illness. Richard had been angry with his brother and had wanted him out of the picture all of his life. His fantasy was now becoming a reality, and on a deep level Richard believed he was murdering his brother, killing him off. He couldn't tolerate this, and his depression and self-punishment increased. One way he punished himself was by driving away his wife, who could have been close to him and useful to him. Because of his guilt he denied himself a warm and loving relationship.

As a result of the crisis he was in, Richard was more forthcoming in his discussions with me. His defenses were less rigid than they would have been without the crisis, and his psyche was in a dynamic rather than a stactic state. I could elicit more from him with less effort than might otherwise have been possible.

In the third session, as I questioned Richard about his sex life, he became extremely resistant and at one point ordered me to stop asking him such questions. I responded by discussing the issue of intimacy between him and me, and I helped him understand that he was trying to avoid being close with me in order to punish himself and sabotage his therapy. At this point, his attitude softened, and after explaining how difficult it was for him, he was able to talk about sex. Again, by challenging his defenses, I elicited material from him that allowed me to be close to him, to share his intimate thoughts.

In the fourth session, he related that he had been very depressed the previous weekend. He had been thinking about his high school guidance counselor, who had been kind to him when he wasn't accepted by the college he wanted to attend. The counselor had taken him to the cafeteria for a cup of coffee and talked to him. This memory brought with it a great deal of sadness, to the extent that he had sobbed as he thought about it. Initially he associated the guidance counselor with his father, with whom he had had a distant relationship. He then linked the emotions he had toward his father with other people he had felt estranged from in his life, his wife in particular. He described at length the mixed feelings he had for her and how he perceived himself as a punitive person.

By taking an inventory of all the emotions he harbored toward his wife, Richard was able to see that anger was not the sole feeling he had for her; it was only one among many. He was able to defuse the intensity of his angry emotions and to bring them into perspective and balance. When he discovered that anger took its place next to sympathy and tender feelings and guilt, the impulses generated by his anger diminished, as did his anxiety about those impulses. During the subsequent weeks, Richard reported that his relationship with his wife became positive and included a greater degree of closeness.

Five Defenses That Can Endanger Your Relationships

There are many reasons why relationships don't work. Often they fail because of the hidden feelings and fears of one or both partners. Because they can be extremely painful to face, these emotions are usually buried.

Unless we become aware of how our buried feelings and fears intrude into our lives, our relationships will remain troubled, and we will continue being perplexed about the reasons. Our defenses can keep us from that awareness. Following is a discussion of how five key defenses work against our success in relationships.

Rationalization

Rationalization is making excuses for why you couldn't go to a social gathering of people who might have been interesting to you, why you forgot your girlfriend's birthday, why you didn't call that nice person back after the first date. Many people rationalize their way through life and relationships, or through a life that lacks relationships.

Anything and everything is grist for the mill of the rationalizer. People who are afraid of their own anger frequently offer rationalizations about why they're not direct and open about their feelings: "I didn't tell her how angry I was because she never listens anyway." The fear of closeness can easily be masked by rationalization: "I don't have a relationship because I can never find the right person. I went out with this guy the other night, and he showed up wearing white socks. He had on the worst sports jacket, and I said to myself, "How could I possibly have anything to say to this guy?" Meanwhile therapists hear from people how desperate they are: "I'm alone"; "I'm sad"; "There's nobody out there."

Many people rationalize their infidelity. They can always find a reason to step outside the boundaries of a relationship, setting the stage for it to deteriorate or disintegrate. Such rationalizations have become platitudes: "My wife doesn't understand me" is almost a joke, but it is still rolled out. "I'm not appreciated" is another rationalization, with a sprinkling of victimization thrown in.

Sexual problems also invite rationalization. Because our culture places a premium on sex, people have a difficult time accepting responsibility when sexual problems exist: "I'm not really that interested in sex"; "She is cool toward me in bed and never asks me to have sex"; "I've been very busy with work"; "Since my mother got sick, I haven't been interested."

Helplessness

An easy way to sabotage a relationship is to take a helpless position. You may become helpless for any number of reasons: a feeling that you aren't entitled to a point of view or that you don't deserve a healthy relationship; a fear of expressing your own anger or becoming truly intimate; anxiety and fear of the unknown. If chronic and prolonged, helplessness can result in an emotional paralysis in which the isolation of thought from feeling is so great that a person is unable to begin new relationships.

One of the most common reasons for taking a helpless stance in a relationship is a desire to get out of it. Perhaps because of mixed emotions you are unable to end a relationship. Instead, you put yourself and your partner through a protracted period of suffering and frustration until finally your partner decides to leave you.

This type of helplessness may be rooted in aggressive impulses; you may actually use the helplessness to elicit a response from your partner. In this way you can passively drive the other person away and then spread your palms outward and take the position of victim, saying, "Look what my partner did to me." Then your friends and relatives can cluck their tongues and lament about how badly you were treated. The truth is that dismantling a relationship by attrition, by eliciting rage and frustration and unhappiness in the other person, is a way of ventilating your anger and hostility.

Avoidance

Going to bed early or staying out with your friends is a form of avoidance, as are working late most nights and getting deeply involved in a hobby. Avoidance is discussing your intimate thoughts and feelings with somebody else, rather than coming home and putting them on the table with your partner. It's looking for attention elsewhere, steering clear of sex and the companionship of the relationship. It's the root of a common complaint: "We don't talk anymore."

Working late, pursuing solitary pastimes, choosing social events that don't require intimacy, like going to the movies or watching television rather than having dinner or just talking—in such situations, interchange and closeness are prevented or limited, and a healthy relationship is not allowed to grow.

The fear of your own anger can sometimes stimulate avoidance. Your fantasy of what you're going to do to the person you're angry with may be so overwhelming—you could destroy them with words, you could strike them or throw them out the window—that you leave the room or go to a movie by yourself. "We don't talk much anymore." Why? Because in talking you run the risk of feeling unpleasant or frightening emotions and acting on them. Besides, avoidance can also be a way of punishing another person.

When your anxiety about sexual problems becomes intense, avoidance is one way to deal with the problem instead of attempting to work it through. Premature ejaculation in a man, lack of orgasm in a woman, upsetting sexual fantasies—all are commonly dealt with by avoidance, which may seem like the easiest "solution" to the problem.

Avoidance readily works in tandem with other defenses. "I don't feel like getting dressed": that's depression and avoidance. "Who wants to hang out with them anyway? They're jerks": that's rationalization and avoidance.

Anger

You can use anger to keep your partner at a distance; if you're angry at that person, you tell yourself that you can't be close. "I was so annoyed that I spent the night out."

Anger is a good way to avoid someone. As an abrupt termination of a difficult discussion, a person may shout, "I don't want to deal with this! Can't I come home and have a peaceful dinner at least one night a week?"

An angry person is not an intimate person. An effective way to avoid sex is to be angry; when you don't want to confront your sexual problems, you can tell yourself that you're too angry to have sex.

Depression

You may use defensive depression as a response to an aspect of a relationship that you can't tolerate. You may have been using depression to hide from a serious problem in your relationship or an unresolved dynamic with your partner.

You may be using depression to keep yourself from getting into a relationship. Self-hate can be so intense and so deeply rooted that you experience it as depression. "I'm so depressed that I don't feel like going out" is a cover for "I hate myself so much that I feel I'm not entitled to a relationship."

Very often depression serves as a protection against anger. Likewise, it can be a way of perpetuating the fear of closeness, an excuse for not becoming intimate with another person. Through defensive depression, you may be protecting yourself from sexual anxieties or some other underlying problem.

Understanding the Process of Relating

We all tend to buy into misperceptions, which we foist upon ourselves in an infinite number of ways. For instance, we want to send a space vehicle into suborbital flight with civilians aboard, so we call it a shuttle. The name implies that, as with a regularly scheduled New York-to-Washington flight, it is predictable and safe. But we have learned, painfully, that it's a rocket ship and it can explode. Most of us harbor misperceptions, in part because we want to believe them. We are especially gullible when it comes to intimate relationships.

Much of the guilt and anger that arise from problems with relationships would dissipate if we could develop an appropriate view of the process of relating. Such a view would center on the idea that painful emotions are a normal ingredient of relationships. As simplistic as this observation seems, most people do not accept it as true. Instead they strive or hope for an idealized relationship, for what they believe a relationship should be. A novel but realistic definition of "relating" would be "a process in which two people interact while simultaneously generating both positive and negative impulses."

We routinely and consistently misperceive the most common issues of our lives. As suggested above, our use of language lends support to these misperceptions. As another example, we apply the word "accident" to events that occur with predictable regularity. Yet, if a given number of automobiles are on the nation's highways on a given day, we can predict the number of collisions that will occur. What is "accidental" about these occurrences? We allow the word "accident" to become further entrenched as a bona fide concept because it carries an emotional connotation.

We use many words that are colored by emotion, further complicating our ability to assess and evaluate the attitudes and beliefs they are meant to describe. The following words are highly charged: "death," "divorce," "cancer," "AIDS," "infidelity," "foreclosure," "heart attack." The difficulty of critically evaluating an idea or a situation is increased when the emotional charge attached to a word is not readily evident. "Relationship" is one such word; "sex" is another.

Sex and relating to another person involve complex

sets of feelings, attitudes, and behavior that ebb and flow. Our desire and ability to relate to someone, sexually or otherwise, does not remain constant and consistent but changes from day to day. However, we ignore this obvious observation and instead perceive sex and relationships in an overvalued and idealized manner. When our experiences fall short of our idealized notions, we feel disappointed and frustrated.

One major misperception is that everybody actively wants an intimate relationship and that everybody wants sex. Magazines, films, and advertisements trade on this misperception. We talk about relationships and sex as though we're all on the same wavelength. Two people are likely to enter a relationship thinking that they both want intimacy and an active sex life. However, because of all the obstacles to relating, it's possible that they don't want these things as much as they tell themselves they do.

This first misperception fosters another: that intimacy and sex are spontaneous and natural, that you don't have to work at them, that, as with a perpetual motion machine, you don't have to put anything into a relationship once you've found the right "chemistry."

Intimacy is hard work. Sex is hard work. If you want a good relationship, you have to work at it. In our society we accept the fact that toning our bodies or running twenty-six miles takes a great deal of effort. If we want success and satisfaction in our careers, we know that hard work and concentrated time and attention are required. Yet we don't understand that it's the same with sex and intimacy. To have a successful love relationship, you and your partner must work very hard at it.

If you have a fear of being close with someone, the initial work lies in admitting your fear and coming to grips with your underlying reasons for resisting closeness. You must look at all the rationalizations that you bring to the situation, the excuses you give yourself for not being around other people. You must learn to deal with the discomfort you feel when you're in a social setting. You fear that your clothes don't fit right, you hate your haircut, you think you look haggard and drawn, you're not a good dancer, you don't have a way with words. Your challenge is to overcome such anxieties and say, "I'm going to do my best." You may also have to work at accepting other people, realizing that a style of dress or other idiosyncracy doesn't reveal all there is to know and appreciate about another human being.

Humans may be social animals because they have to work and associate with other people out of basic self-interest, but that doesn't mean that they are by nature intimate animals. For thousands of years, people have successfully banded together for protection and survival, but all of them don't bond intimately with the same degree of success. People marry for many reasons—because they want to have children, because they want to share expenses with another person, or because they love someone—but true intimacy is the result of hard work.

Working at intimacy means acknowledging and sharing with another person your intimate thoughts. It means running the risk of eliciting from the other person an unwelcome response. You have to learn to live with the anxieties that can go along with a sexual encounter. But, as with physical exercise, the more you do it the easier it becomes. You can develop intimacy to the point where you can say something to your partner and have total trust that, no matter what you say, the response is going to be an accepting one, an understanding one.

Sex is hard work. It means taking time out from your busy schedule, from the obligations of your life. It means doing something that's totally reserved for you and your partner. It has nothing to do with the children, with your work or business, with painting the house or watching that TV program you both want to see. It has to do with just the two of you. Sometimes having good sex involves setting priorities and making choices, and all too often it's easier not to make that choice, to let your sexual relationship slide, and to rationalize why you let it slide.

The partners in a sexual relationship must pay attention to the content of the sex itself. Repetitive sex, like repetitive anything, is boring. It's not just a matter of reading a guidebook. You must take time and put energy into reaffirming your interest in this other human being. The popular illusion is that, once you're with somebody you love, sex will be wonderful, intimacy will be there forever, trust will be there, no matter what. But this idea really is an illusion.

Two important first steps in achieving a close personal relationship are to try to avoid misperceptions and to set aside unexamined assumptions. A further step is to accept the idea that you are responsible for your life and for the success or failure of your relationships. Becoming more emotionally honest means becoming more critical and more aware of your defenses, more interested in the problems and circumstances that lie below the surface of your life.

CHAPTER 7

Subverting Success at Work

Your behavior at work may exhibit strong parallels to the way you act in relationships. What you bring to a relationship—how you deal with your defenses, the way you ignore or confront your painful, buried feelings—you also bring to your work. And, as in relationships, your degree of self-awareness on your job will make it a losing or a winning endeavor.

Paying for the Past

Alan, a man in his forties, entered therapy when his life came crashing down around him.

Alan's father had been a butcher who drank and gambled with the money his shop brought in. When Alan was sixteen, his father lost his business. Alan left school to work and support the family, letting his mother effectively elevate him to the status of man of the house; together they "neutralized" his father. Instead of remaining close to his father, Alan cut him out. In our first therapy session, he told me that he felt nothing but a sense of inconvenience when his father died.

At the time he came into therapy, Alan's business, a car dealership, had fallen on hard times as a result of bad business decisions. Alan was forced to take in partners and reduce his income. He was denied a position of authority and received a salary.

In therapy, Alan was concerned about saving his marriage. He described his wife as judgmental.

Alan: My wife says we are penniless. I did not take care of her.

Zois: How do you feel as you recall her statement to you?

Alan: I tell her that for years I was a good provider. [rationalization]

Zois: So you explain yourself.

Alan: Yes.

Zois: However, you have not told me how you feel.

Alan: It makes me angry. [anger]

Zois: Do you declare your anger?

Alan: No.

Zois: How else do you feel when you hear these things from your wife, because as you tell them to me you appear other than angry.

Alan: It hurts my feelings that she is not supportive during this hard time.

Zois: Do you tell her this?

Alan: No. [avoidance]

Zois: So you hide all your feelings and keep your distance from her.

Alan: What good would it do? [intellectualization]

Zois: Do you see how you take a helpless victim position with her and, by indulging in explanations and other surface conversations, invite even more criticism? There is a part of you that wants to continue to suffer. If you didn't want to suffer, you wouldn't embrace the role of a martyr who is abused by what he calls an ungrateful, uncaring wife.

Alan's underlying problem was guilt. He acknowledged that whenever things were going well, he always thought, "It shouldn't be happening. I shouldn't make out this well." His story is a profile of a man who carried intensely mixed feelings. His buried thought that he had cheated his father gave rise to a self-punishing sense of guilt, which he acted out in running his business. On a deep level, his goals had always been to suffer in atonement for the death of his father and to end his life as his father had, on the sidelines and without resources.

Besides rationalization, anger, avoidance, and intellectualization, another key defense that Alan used was denial. During the initial evaluation, we had discussed Alan's relationship with his mother and father and examined the similarities between his life and his father's. In the sixth session, he told me that his wife had come home from her therapist with some interesting "news." She and her therapist had discussed Alan, and her therapist had made an interpretation similiar to mine: that Alan was reliving his father's life. Even though Alan and I had discussed this parallel in our initial session as well as in the two subsequent sessions, he declared that this was new information.

Denial can be a potent way of dealing with material that causes discomfort or pain. With some individuals, I have to go over material time and again, making certain that they have allowed it into their awareness. And, of course, Alan's denial had to be addressed in his therapy. He had stated that his associates often told him he didn't "hear well"—a convenient way to ignore information and advice and to maintain a nonproductive course of action.

When his business failed and he sat in defeat, Alan's wife wouldn't let up on him. In therapy, he came to understand that he had "created" a judgmental wife for himself in order to perpetuate his punishment. Over the years he had fostered her spending habits, which were now causing a great deal of friction in the marriage. Also, he had teamed up with his mother against his wife and in many ways had treated her like an outsider.

His wife had become angry and nagging, punitive and lecturing, and Alan dealt with her frustration and anger only on a surface level, thereby allowing it to continue. By perpetuating his anger he was able to defend himself successfully against closeness with her, rationalizing that it was impossible to be intimate with an ungrateful woman. He had enraged and frustrated his wife with his "long-suffering" behavior and attitudes. He also had allowed her to think that he constantly needed to be guided and directed.

Alan eventually faced the self-sabotaging impulses he had directed against himself. Once he examined his guilt and his lifelong desire to punish himself, he was able to take action. He discarded the role of victim and established a closer and more caring relationship with his wife. He stopped causing himself to suffer needlessly.

Trapped in a Mind-set

Although she held an important position and earned a good salary, Janice was unhappy in her work as an advertising executive. She felt her superiors didn't appreciate her contributions, and she was dissatisfied with her colleagues, who in her view were pleasant and cooperative enough but lacked energy, responsibility, and imagination. She saw herself as carrying the entire department.

Recently divorced, Janice had no significant relationships in her life. During our initial session, she spoke of difficulties with her family, describing herself as an outsider who always came up short in comparison with her sister, whom her parents favored. Janice's father owned a manufacturing concern, and her sister worked with him. With her husband and children, she lived in the town where she had always lived, down the block from her parents; the two households had dinner together at least once a week, spent part of each weekend together, and often went on vacations together.

Janice, on the other hand, had gone into advertising and, without any family ties to back her up, made a successful career. She lived in the city and didn't spend as much time with her parents as her sister did. Janice saw herself as having paid a price for her success; in her mind she was being punished by the family for not being as close to them as her sister was.

Janice felt so cheated that she was very resistant to acknowledging any positive elements in her relationship with her family; when positive events occurred, she would assign them either a negative or an indifferent interpretation. One of her complaints was that her sister was the recipient of all monetary and emotional benefits provided by her parents, that she herself got nothing. Yet she related that during one visit her mother took her into the bedroom and gave her a family heirloom, a brooch that had belonged to her grandmother, saying, "Janice, I want you to have this." Janice and I discussed this incident.

Zois: How do you feel that your mother gave you the brooch?

Janice: I thought, "Boy, my sister is really going to be angry if she finds out about this." [avoidance]

Janice then talked about how she believed her sister would feel rather than responding to the question about her own emotion toward her mother.

Zois: That's a description. You haven't told me how you feel.

Janice: Well, it was a nice thing for my mother to do.

Zois: That's another description. How do you feel that your mother gave you something that's very valuable to her.

Janice: I feel good.

Zois: You notice that it's difficult for you to acknowledge those good feelings.

After this discussion I knew that I needed to have Janice focus on her hostility toward her sister. A part of Janice wanted her sister to be angry, in the same way that Janice herself was angry about all the things she perceived her sister to have received.

Only after extensive dialogue was Janice able to acknowledge that the gift was an illustration of her mother's tender feelings toward her. She resisted giving up the victim role and had great difficulty integrating the good memories from her past into her perception of her parents and sister. Such resistance is not uncommon. With many patients I have to focus on such material again and again—and deal with defense after defense—before the good memories are integrated into an ongoing perception of the family or spouse or friends.

Janice was locked in a certain mind-set—resentment at a feeling of being cheated—and that mind-set affected many situations in her life. Janice had transferred her feelings about her family to her work situation.

After we sorted out her mixed feelings toward her family, she was able to look at her work in a more objective light and find satisfying elements in it that she couldn't acknowledge before. Once she was able to develop a realistic view of her colleagues, she saw herself as less burdened and not the only responsible person in her department. The people around her seemed to be contributing more. She recognized that her description of herself as the only one who carried the ball was similar to the way she had seen herself within her family: as a productive, independent adult whose parents did not acknowledge her achievement.

Part of Janice's new sense of satisfaction was her ability to acknowledge positive events and feelings. For a person with a negative mind-set, clarifying the origin of problem issues allows the mind-set to dissipate. When Janice began to view people in a more balanced way, she was able to see what they were contributing.

Janice also reported that she was getting more positive feedback at work. She had apparently begun to covertly and overtly communicate a different sense of who she was. We all author the response of others toward us. After someone like Janice comes to an awareness that breaks a negative mind-set, she gives off a different vibe, or a different karma. People view her differently. Janice reported that she felt more approachable and in turn approached people more easily. She was able to enjoy her work rather than feel burdened by it.

Something else happened to help Janice out of her self-defeating mind-set. She came to accept a key statement, which I have discussed in connection with guilt: "That's the way it is." Her father and her mother were the way they were; Janice couldn't change them. They responded to attention and to a sense of close family unity. Janice needed to come to grips with the fact that she had to pay a price for leaving the tightly knit family group. Leaving didn't mean that she couldn't care about her family and have them care about her, but she wouldn't receive the rewards she might have if she had lived in their emotional backyard.

You do not undergo a process of emotional change in order to alter the responses of the people around you. The insights and awareness that you come to are on your own behalf, for yourself alone. It's possible that people may accommodate to the new you, and when that happens it's gratifying and rewarding. However, the goal of emotional change is not to be a hostage to the responses and attitudes of others; it is to be emotionally self-sufficient in terms of your own sense of well-being.

In Janice's case, no accommodation from her parents was forthcoming. They did not share her philosophical and emotional point of view, and the best she could do was to develop a tolerance for their attitudes. However, she had accomplished a sense of her own self-worth in the face of their judgmental behavior.

A Whiner and a Quitter

Jack was an accountant who bounced from job to job because his response to confrontation was to blame others and then to quit. Jack told me about a conversation he had with a couple of co-workers on his current job, as they were gathered at the fax machine.

Jack: I don't know why the boss is always on me about deadlines. You can't rush this type of audit—it takes time!

Dave: He's a bulldog all right.

Joann: What's the problem with your audit, Jack?

Jack: You know, the usual. This crazy client is always coming up with a new box of documents that I have to deal with, and their books look like someone with a crayon made the entries.

Dave: Sounds familiar.

Joann: Have you told the boss about the reasons for the delay?

Jack: Ah, what's the use? He never cuts me any slack.

Joann: But you know how incensed he gets if we miss deadlines.

Jack: Let him. I'm about ready to kiss this job good-bye anyway.

We picked up the thread of that conversation in Jack's next therapy session.

Jack: So I said to them that if he gave me any trouble about the deadline, I'd show him—I'd quit!

Zois: You want to deal with your anger by avoidance.

Jack: Nobody there appreciates me anyway. Joann's a nice kid, but she doesn't understand; she's too interested in kowtowing to the boss. And that guy Dave, with his enigmatic little one-liners. I always feel like he's judging me.

Zois: So it's still "poor little me."

Jack: Well, what am I supposed to do?

Zois: So you're helpless—an angry, victimized, helpless cripple. How do you feel that you present yourself here to me as limp?

Jack: What do you mean?

Zois: What I mean is that you come here and you tell me you're a cripple, you want to be a victim the rest of your life. If you would be honest with yourself, you'd see that your anger and your intellectualizing about where you are in life and how smart you are and where you deserve to be has gotten you nowhere. Isn't that the fact? And you sabotage yourself on every job. You are a self-hating, sabotaging human being. If you would be very honest with yourself, isn't that the way it is?

Jack: Well, I don't think so.

Zois: So you want to sit here and talk about what you think and don't think, but you don't want to look at where you are. When you first came in, you told me you haven't gotten anywhere in your work; this is your third job. Isn't it the truth that you are nowhere in your work and you want to hide behind victimization and rationalization and anger? Isn't that the way it is? The same way you want to hide behind that with me here, to keep a wall between the two of us, so I'll just be one other person you can talk about, just like your boss and Joann and Dave. A nice understanding guy, but he had no impact. So what's going to happen if we go on like this together?

Jack: Well, nothing.

Zois: So why do you want to do that to yourself? You're a young man, you have your life ahead of you, but you're behaving as if you don't want anything for yourself.

I always tailor my approach to the degree of resistance the patient exhibits. Jack was a very resistant person. In his conversations with his co-workers, he had all the defenses in place—avoidance, anger, helplessness, intellectualization. It was important that I confront these defenses in a global, summary way. I enumerated them and then used his own words to describe where he was in life. Lastly, as I did with Charles, I appealed directly to the part of him that wanted to change.

Jack's statements about his job revealed how he felt about himself in general: that no one had ever understood him. As Jack talked about his life, he related countless incidents in which he saw himself as an unappreciated figure.

Unfortunately, his self-perception was echoed in other people's responses to him. The reply the boss (and the world) had to Jack's self-absorbed and self-pitying statements was "So what?" People intuited the broader meaning that Jack's defensiveness and behavior conveyed, and typically experienced a sense of irritation toward him. His excellent work was eclipsed by his negative, complaining attitude.

Jack told himself, "Feeling unappreciated is a way of life for me. Because of this I will never find a place where my talents are recognized." Jack continued to interact with his superiors and co-workers in an unsatisfying and unrewarded way until he modified his helplessness and avoidance and came face to face with the hurt he felt from other people.

Until he took action to leave his defenses behind and confront his hurt, Jack continued to frustrate his desire for success at work. Because he presented himself as an ineffectual whiner, he activated the natural impatience most people feel toward chronically discontented people. We want them to go away because their attitudes remind us of feelings we ourselves have had to struggle to overcome; we don't want to be infected by the same disease. Jack needed to understand that his behavior and attitudes were triggering the fears of others around him, that he was communicating in a way that worked against him.

When Jack penetrated his defenses and became aware of the covert messages transmitted by his moaning and groaning, he started to make his statements more positive. In the past he would have said to his boss, "You're a fool—I quit." Instead he became able to say, "I want to effectively utilize the firm's assets, and I hope the firm will utilize mine. I want to find ways to increase my contribution."

He was still able to express his dissatisfaction, but he did so in an acceptable way while making an effective statement about himself as well. Instead of a whining complainer, Jack is now perceived as a man in control of his life, one who is able to make objective assessments of situations even when they affect him personally. Rather than a person filled with inadequacies, he now comes across as someone who is not afraid to identify and own up to difficulties, someone willing to assume responsibility when things go wrong as well as when things go right.

Jack no longer has to lie about how he really feels in order to project an acceptable image of himself. He is able to express dissatisfaction honestly, but now his statements don't denigrate himself or others. He therefore inspires confidence instead of fear, and his co-workers can relate to him in comfort. He no longer activates their fears, anxieties, and inadequacies. Because they don't feel threatened by his statements of dissatisfaction, they can afford to pay attention to him and give his ideas credence. They can evaluate his statements objectively rather than ignoring them as noise emanating from a chronic complainer.

If you're guilt-ridden, you're going to bring some degree of lack of entitlement and self-sabotage to your work. If you distance yourself from people in your personal life, there is a good chance that you're going to act the same way at work. If you react to situations with defensive anger, your work life will be affected by that unexamined rage.

Here are some defenses that you might hear around just about any water cooler.

- "If he can't see what I've done for this firm, the hell with him." [anger]
- "They're in my way. How can you get anywhere when you're always being stabbed in the back?" [rationalization]
- "Who needs them?" [avoidance]
- "I just don't know what to do to advance up the corporate ladder." [helplessness]
- "I've been manning the same desk for twelve years now. True, it's a little boring sometimes, but basically I'm happy." [denial]
- "What can you do in this economic environment?" [intellectualization]

There can be subtle differences, of course. Because relationships at work are perceived as safer than intimate relationships, the defenses that we use to keep our intimate or personal relationships at arm's length may not be the same defenses we use at work. For example, it's not uncommon to encounter a man who is cold as a father and husband but who functions as a captain of industry. Such a dichotomy may exist because the person's self-sabotage is limited to the realm of intimacy and doesn't have much to do with worldly success. Furthermore, people often avoid intimacy by displacing their psychic energy onto work. Such people go through the mechanics of having a home and a family but in fact sleepwalk through their relationships; the only time they are alive is when they're working.

Then there are people who have substituted their work for a relationship. Viewed as a kind of relationship, work is very safe. It's the same kind of relationship one can have to alcohol. It's possible to turn with confidence to work because, unlike personal relationships, it won't let you down. Work doesn't carry the risk of the psychic pain of rejection or abandonment. For some people, then, work is a way to avoid intimacy.

Some people enter therapy when the defenses that operate in their relationships begin to interfere with their work as well. More often than not, those who are self-sabotaging in their relationships will sabotage themselves at work, too.

Your achievements or shortcomings at work are more quantifiable than your successes and failures in relationships. As a result, it can be easy for you to see when you are "acting out" at work your conflicts about your deep emotions and impulses.

For example, it's relatively easy to spot your defensiveness if you hear yourself say, "I'm smarter than my boss. Why the hell is he in charge while I'm sitting here pushing pencils?" In terms of intelligence, perhaps you are smarter than your boss, but so what? If you ask that question in an attempt to take stock of where you are, that's fine, but if you ask it out of anger, then it's just a rationalization, an excuse for not doing what you need to do in order to succeed. In addition, your attitude is distancing; it feeds into victimization and a sense of being cheated. Instead of thinking about running the company and how cheated you are, you should be thinking about what you can do to reach the next rung up on the professional ladder.

People who say "I'm smarter than my boss" are usually not taking stock. They usually say it as a way to experience victimization and seething unrest and anger. These defenses do not promote a productive relationship with superiors or anyone else. They often cover a profound desire for self-sabotage.

We hear a great deal about the mid-life crisis, which is generally defined as a crisis about facing your mortality. That's true to a degree, but there's more to it. In my patients who suffer from a so-called mid-life crisis I see a need to pay for their guilt, a realization that they have not atoned for the suffering they've caused.

In Chapter 5, I described the "agony of success," the inner desperation experienced by people who feel they are not entitled to succeed but who have become successful anyway. Such people are racked by discomfort. For one reason or another, their attempts at self-sabotage have not worked. They admit that they weren't happy with life as it was, so they dropped out: "I was chairman of the board, but now I belong to a motorcycle club" or "I no longer saw the value in being a nuclear physicist." Their urge to sabotage themselves notwithstanding, these people succeeded in life, and they couldn't stand it. So they walked away, to take up hang gliding or to write the Great American Novel. Those who do stay on the job sometimes make a crucial error of judgment or do something gratuitously foolish.

It's usually a mistake to attempt to view one aspect of your life out of the context of the rest of your existence. It's like trying to understand a book by reading only one chapter. As a rule, our relationships at work are replications of the ones we have with our spouses, lovers, parents, siblings, and friends. If we allow our hidden emotions to hold sway in our lives in general, they will determine how we view the work environment, how we relate to colleagues and co-workers, and how we see ourselves. If instead we consistently strip away our defenses and get a clear view of what's going on at our deepest emotional level, we will be able to approach our work free of self-sabotage, negative mind-sets, unresolved anger, and the other encumbrances that arise from unresolved problems.

CHAPTER 8

The Most Difficult Word: "Good-bye"

The ability to say good-bye is one of the cornerstones of mental health. Your ongoing ability to tolerate losses of all kinds—death, divorce, altered circumstances, a change of jobs, retirement, a loss of money, estrangement from someone close to you—is determined by your past experiences of loss, including those that occurred in your earliest years, as well as the way you deal with your strong emotions—anger, hurt, and guilt.

The most constant experience in life is change, and we very often equate change with loss. We change locales, we graduate from school, we say good-bye to kind teachers, to good friends, to the old neighborhood. It is very important to be able to live through this continuing series of changes in a way that does not leave a residue of pain, sadness, depression, and grief. Such emotions can color our view of future relationships. They can set up a negative cycle that hampers our ability to get the most out of life.

Determined to Be Alone

At age sixty-three, Lily had lost her husband, who died after being ill with cancer for eight months. The marriage had been a good one. The following is a typical telephone conversation between Lily and her married daughter, Susan.

Lily: Hello. I haven't heard from you in several days, so I thought I'd better call.

Susan: I'm sorry I haven't phoned, Mom, but I've been pulled in fourteen different directions. This is the busy season at my job, I've been helping Bill get ready for a big business trip, and the annual ballet recital is coming up for the kids. How have you been?

Lily: How can I be? I have nothing to do. All my friends are married. Even if I wanted to go out, I have nowhere to go.

Susan: I don't know why you say that, Mom.

Lily: I don't expect you to understand what it's like for me now that your father is no longer here. You have your husband and children and your own interests.

Susan: What about the Burkes? You said they wanted you to go into the city with them for the day.

Lily: They're just trying to be nice. They don't really want me along. I'll just stay home and watch my soap operas.

Susan: Mom, that's silly. You know you just get down in the dumps if you stay in the house all day. Didn't you say that Alice Wolf wanted you to join her when she goes walking in the mornings?

Lily: It's fine for you to give advice. How can you know how I feel?

Susan: Maybe you're right, Mom. I wish I could do something to help you feel better.

Lily: An invitation once in a while would be nice.

Susan: I'd love to see you, Mom, but this week is out of the question. Could we make it the middle of next week?

Lily: Oh, never mind. You know, Susan, you really hurt me sometimes.

Susan: Mom, you know I love you...(Lily hangs up.)

Lily was having trouble fitting in with her old friends. She had also begun to feel slighted by her daughter, and she constantly argued with and complained to her. Her daughter was frustrated and consequently tended to avoid her, and that made Lily feel even more rejected. She resented her daughter, who had a husband and a full life. Their relationship was strained, and Lily felt like a bad mother.

Here's an interchange Lily and I had in one of her therapy sessions.

Lily: All of my friends are married and I feel out of place. [avoidance] Even if I wanted to go out, I have nowhere to go. [rationalization]

Zois: But let's look at some of the things that you might do. (We then discussed the options Lily has for a social life.) Really you're just rationalizing and offering excuses about why you continue to isolate yourself and suffer.

Lily: (Loudly) I'm not rationalizing. [anger]

Zois: You raise your voice. How do you feel about my pointing out that you want to continue to suffer?

Lily: I know it's your job to make me think about things.

Zois: That reality doesn't help the way you feel.

Lily: You make me angry. You think it's so easy. It's okay for you to say that. How old are you? You probably have a wife and family. What do you know about being alone? (She starts to cry.) [weepiness]

Zois: You want to put tears in between you and me.

Lily: I don't know what else to do. [helplessness]

Zois: Now you take a helpless position. You say, "I don't know." Do you behave like this with other people?

Lily: Probably. [vagueness]

Zois: You say "probably." Do you or don't you?

Lily: I do.

Zois: With who?

Lily: I guess my daughter.

Zois: You guess?

Lily: My daughter.

Zois: What are your thoughts about your daughter?

Lily: She doesn't understand. She has a husband and children. It's fine for her to give advice.

Zois: How do you feel about the fact that she has someone and you don't?

Lily: Don't misunderstand. I want the best for her.

Zois: But how do you feel?

Lily: I get angry with her sometimes.

Zois: So you resent that she has a husband and you don't.

Lily: I never looked at it that way. I did so much for her. I gave her everything, and now she can't extend herself for me.

Zois: But we're speaking here of your resentment that she has a husband and you don't.

Lily: I don't like to think about that.

Zois: What comes to your mind?

Lily: I get very angry sometimes.

Zois: How angry.

Lily: Sometimes I picture her in my shoes.

Zois: How do you feel about that?

Lily: I hate myself. Those are terrible moments.

Zois: So you suffer with those thoughts and use them to punish yourself.

Lily used an array of defenses in maintaining that a life of isolation and self-punishment was the only one for her. In truth, Lily's reason for not going out, for not enjoying herself, had to do with her emotional reaction to her husband's death. During his illness, Lily had been plagued by the thought that her husband might linger on and become a burden to her. She found herself fearing that his illness would deplete their savings and that, after he died, she would be not only alone but without resources. After he was gone, Lily tortured herself with the thought that a part of her might have wanted her husband to die.

Thoughts and fears such as Lily had are common and normal. Confronted with her husband's illness, she had an honest thought: life would be easier if he were to die. What Lily failed to realize was that this thought did not diminish or detract from the love she had for him. But after he died, Lily suffered guilt and began punishing herself for something that was not her fault—his death. She wanted to suffer. Since her husband had died, Lily believed on a deep level that she did not deserve to live and that, if she had to go on living, she should not have an enjoyable life.

Like Charles, Lily needed to acknowledge and accept her mixed feelings about a past event. One part of her resented the burden her dying husband represented or, as Charles said, "the fact that I was put upon." Faced with caring for her husband and facing a future without him, she had normal responses. Charles felt great rage toward his stepfather, but he also "felt for him" because he was "such a pathetic person that how could I have such rage against this guy?"

Like Charles in his relationship with his stepfather, Lily was in a universal dilemma. She loved her husband, and yet she felt burdened by him. She didn't understand how normal her feelings were, that they were part of the human condition, that they didn't detract from her affection for her husband. Instead, she felt that she must suffer for them.

Lily was unable to confront the guilt she felt, but it plagued her nonetheless. She came up with all sorts of reasons why she couldn't go out with friends, and she used other defenses to ward off challenges to her rationalizations.

When her defenses were stripped away, Lily examined her guilt feelings and came to understand that her fears and feelings were not monstrous but normal. She saw that, in her sorrow at her husband's death and her fear of the future, she had assumed a disproportionate amount of guilt. After an honest and focused reassessment of her past and present feelings, she was able to take action. She began to lead an independent social life, and she resumed a good relationship with her daughter. She was able to let go of her sad past, live in the present, and look forward to the future.

A Flawed Good-bye

Tony was a forty-two-year-old engineer who had been out of work for a year after being fired from a job in which he had had a great deal of responsibility. He had used almost all of his savings—he was down to his last mortgage payment—before he found another position. While unemployed, Tony felt vulnerable and helpless, both financially and emotionally. Getting fired and being out of work for so long had changed his image of himself: he was no longer the decisive, confident man he had once been.

In his new job with a large firm, he reported to a boss who was unreasonable and punitive. Without too much effort, Tony could have transferred to another department, and yet he stayed where he was, even though he knew he wouldn't get promoted and was continually enraged at his new boss.

Tony's anger with his boss echoed feelings he had had as an adolescent toward his father, whom he also saw as a punitive, authoritarian man. Tony had had a complicated relationship with his father, who had died several years before. During his childhood, his parents had fought a lot, and Tony typically sided with his mother, thus alienating himself from his father. Later, when his father became ill and Tony oversaw his medical care, the two men became closer than they had ever been.

Despite the closeness they had achieved, their last visit had ended in a disagreement, and that episode remained with Tony as a symbol of the discord between him and his father.

Zois: When was the last time you saw your father?

Tony: The night he died.

Zois: What did you say to him then?

Tony: He had been feeling bad, and he wanted to go to the hospital. There was a screwup in getting him a hospital bed, and my mother and I got into an argument about what happened. She was saying it was my fault we didn't get him in, and I was saying it was her fault. And he yells, "Shut up."

Zois: Who did he yell at?

Tony: At me. I didn't say anything. I was sitting in the kitchen; he was in the family room. I just kept eating. We had the argument and all. But then I didn't go over and kiss him when I said good night, which was something I'd started doing in the recent past and that he really liked. I didn't go over and kiss him, and then he died that night.

Zois: What was your thought when you didn't go over and kiss him?

Tony: That he rejected me, because he had yelled at me.

Zois: How were you feeling toward him at that moment?
Tony: I felt that he yelled at me because he was on medication and very ill. [rationalization]
Zois: You rationalize that it was the medication and his illness that caused him to yell at you, but still you didn't go kiss him.
Tony: No.
Zois: So how were you feeling toward him?
Tony: I guess angry that he yelled at me. [vagueness]
Zois: You say "I guess."
Tony: I was angry with him.
Zois: When you left to go home, what did you say to him?
Tony: Good night.

Shortly after Tony got home, his mother called: "You'd better come—your father's having a heart attack." By the time he got back to his parents' home, his father had died.

After some discussion of the details of the death, I asked Tony about the funeral.

Zois: What was the funeral like?
Tony: (Pause) It was terrible.
Zois: You say it was terrible. What was terrible about it?
Tony: (Long pause) I can't talk about that. [avoidance]
Zois: How do you feel right now?
Tony: Distraught.
Zois: Have you thought about the funeral before?
Tony: Yes.
Zois: Have you ever discussed this with anybody?
Zois: No. (His eyes fill with tears.)
Zois: So you've kept your feelings locked up.
Tony: Yes.
Zois: Have you cried about it when you were alone?
Tony: Yes.
Zois: What was terrible about that day?
Tony: He was dead.

Zois: What were your thoughts then?

Tony: (Long pause) I had failed to keep him alive.

When the last meeting with someone important contains distressing elements, grief and the ensuing guilt are more intense and prolonged. On a deep, hidden level, Tony harbored the primal thought "I have murdered my father"— but not just because he didn't kiss him or get him into the hospital that day, although those events made his guilt worse.

Tony's guilt was rooted even deeper, in the entire history of the relationship, particularly the way he had distanced himself from his father and sided with his mother against him years ago. The idea of not keeping his father alive was so powerful because he believed that he had cheated him over the course of their lives. Although the two had become closer, the failure to kiss his father good-bye on the night he died allowed Tony to reiterate and accentuate his self-imposed sentence of guilt. Like many people in his situation, Tony judged the lifetime of a relationship by its last hours.

During the years that followed his father's death, Tony was unable to resolve the complicated relationship. The task had been made harder by the assault on his psyche caused by the loss of his job and being unemployed. In his new job, he punished himself and kept himself in a beaten position.

A supportive approach to Tony's dilemma would not have worked. It wouldn't have helped to say to him, "Oh, your father understood." He probably didn't understand: he liked being kissed, and Tony didn't kiss him. It was Tony's last opportunity to show his father affection, and he didn't do it. He has to live with that reality. What should he do? Not kiss his wife and kids? Become isolated and miserable because he wants to perpetuate that blunder? Of course not. But his unresolved guilt continued to affect his life in ways he didn't understand.

Tony had worked for a punitive man whom he disliked so much that he fantasized throwing him out the window. What kept him in that job was his ambivalence, a state of mind that is the product of chronic defensiveness. He knew that he should leave, but his guilt and resulting desire to sabotage himself made him stay. But ambivalence is more than just self-sabotage; by definition it involves mixed feelings. If Tony left the job, he would be letting go of a situation that reminded him of his relationship with his father when he was growing up; staying allowed him to replay the past that was the source of his guilt and to be punished for it at the same time.

Once he understood and modified his isolation and defenses (rationalizations, vagueness, avoidance), Tony was able to experience the painful emotions surrounding his relationship with his father. As he took an inventory of them, he was able to put the feelings generated by the relationship in perspective and to identify his ambivalence and his self-sabotaging behavior. Having reassessed his perception of his guilt, he was able to minimize the self-defeating impulse and to channel his emotional energy in a more productive and satisfying way.

Divorced and Enraged

After a seven-year marriage, Bob informed Jane that he didn't love her anymore, and he moved out. They had no children. Jane soon learned through friends that Bob was dating another woman. Within a couple of months, he sued for divorce.

At age thirty-five, Jane was very angry and unhappy with her life. After the breakup, she had several short-lived sexual relationships, and some of the men treated her badly. Yet she continued the pattern, often finding herself in sexual situations with men she really didn't like or respect. She was trying to reinforce her self-image as a sexually attractive woman, but she was doing so in a way that was filled with complications and that in fact had the opposite effect.

Jane couldn't get over Bob. She continued to experience overwhelming rage and anger toward him. Here's what happened in one therapy session as we discussed the conversation in which Bob told Jane he wanted a divorce.

Zois: What was your feeling when Bob said these things to you?

Jane: How could he do this after all these years?

Zois: That's a question. What's your emotion as you think about that discussion right now.

Jane: I feel like crying. [weepiness]

Zois: What is the emotion under those tears?

Jane: I feel very sad. I feel very hurt.

Zois: What is the emotion under that hurt?

Jane: You mean anger?

Zois: That word comes to your mind. Are you angry with him?

Jane: Yes, I told you that before. [She had discussed her rage fantasies earlier in the session.]

Zois: How do you feel right now?

Jane: I feel like a jerk, humiliated. I haven't dared admit it to anyone.

Zois: You call yourself names in an attempt to avoid looking at the emotion that you describe—anger.

Because Jane feels intense rage at her husband for treating her unkindly when he wanted to end their marriage, I deal with her sadness and hurt as defenses against her anger.

Often patients get a sense of what the therapist is looking for. Jane offers what she thinks is a revelation about herself: "I feel like a jerk, humiliated." If Jane had used different language in an appropriate context—for example, if she had said, "I am filled with a sense of shame," and if her face had reflected that kind of emotion—I would have examined her statement. But because of the way she related to me and her choice of words ("jerk"), I elected to treat her statements as a defensive maneuver rather than as an expression of authentic emotion. (The therapist faces a similar decision when a patient is being weepy as opposed to having authentic feelings of grief.)

Instead of getting sidetracked into a discussion of intimacy with her, I stay with the focus, because in this instance she's using intimacy to stay away from the anger. The therapist must guard against being seduced by comments that in another context might be valid but that in the present context are merely defensive. (Something similar happened with Charles. As we were talking about his brother, he brought up his stepfather. I told him, "We'll get to your stepfather." I put him on notice that we would eventually cover everything, but that first we would cover the issues at hand.)

After Jane faced her strong feelings of anger and came to grips with them, we dealt with her authentic feelings of hurt and sadness at the loss of Bob. We had to deal first with the feeling that was bothering her the most—the overwhelming anger that she hadn't been able to come to terms with.

Divorce or the breakup of a relationship can be viewed as tantamount to a death. Frequently the reality of the separation is colored by confusing it, emotionally, with a death.

When someone leaves you, you may lose your self-esteem: he or she does not want you but prefers somebody else. That can be very painful and can profoundly shake your confidence. Sexuality is linked to self-esteem. "He prefers another woman. I am not desirable. I will never make any man happy. What will become of me?" The person who is left fears being viewed as deviant, demented, unfit. Frequently family members offer criticism rather than support: "How could you have allowed him to leave?" In other words, maybe there is something wrong with you. Then there's financial loss. Today, because many families depend on two salaries, financial troubles accompany most divorces.

Given all the things that you confront in a divorce or separation, how do you deal with it? At such a time, your hidden feelings and impulses play a particularly large role, and you must honestly scrutinize what you are feeling. Being able to do that depends on avoiding the defenses.

Jane came to understand that she was extremely angry and that her anger and her feelings of being helpless and victimized were defenses that worked against her best interests. By analyzing and challenging these defenses, she was able to take inventory of the conflicting emotions that she experienced when Bob left her. Jane had an intense emotional reaction to what she perceived as her humiliation. Experiencing the pain that accompanied it allowed her to see other situations in which she had handed herself over to someone. When she understood that this behavior had caused her more unhappiness than success, she was able to make changes.

She stopped speaking to Bob directly and dealt with him only through her attorney. She moved out of the apartment they had shared and into one that held no memories. Jane could not have accomplished these changes if she hadn't broken through her defenses, thus allowing her to see what she was doing to herself and to experience what that view of herself felt like emotionally. She felt the pain directly and took measures to avoid such distress in the future.

Why It's Hard to Say Good-bye

Because it is natural to avoid painful feelings and impulses, we often resort to mental attitudes and types of behavior that shield or distract us from the true feelings a loss provokes. This is rather like putting off a trip to the dentist because you fear the pain. Whether you employ defenses, and to what degree, largely depends on how much emotional pain you feel, and the degree of pain is influenced by three major factors.

One is your past experience. In your mind, do you identify a loved one who has recently died with someone you lost in the past? Does a loss remind you of something that happened in your childhood? One of my patients couldn't tolerate the idea of relocating, even though it was to a very good situation, because he associated it with a depressing event in his childhood, when his family had been forced to move to a less affluent neighborhood. He went so far as to project those same emotions onto his children, even though they had no problem with moving. As another example, a person who loses a pet might experience huge grief if the pet's love represents the unconditional love of a parent who died when the person was young or the kind of love he or she craved but never received.

A second factor is the history of the relationship or the experience—how much guilt was involved, how many mixed feelings existed, how many bad feelings there were. "After Ellen died, I kept thinking back to the time when I had an affair. She was so unhappy." Or "Ever since Al left me, I've been thinking about how he always wanted to be an artist. I insisted he go to law school, and he never liked being a lawyer." If one feels guilt or deep regret about certain aspects of a relationship or situation, these feelings can give rise to defenses that perpetuate self-sabotaging behavior.

A third factor is the guilt many people experience, along with other painful emotions, in connection with a loss. In the case of a death, these feelings can be exaggerated into a sense of having participated in or caused the death, and therefore they can give rise to all kinds of inaccurate and pointless recriminations. "I listened to that doctor, but we should have gone to Boston, where Joe would have had open-heart surgery." Or "Jean was complaining of chest pains. I knew she wasn't feeling well, and yet I selfishly went out with my friends." Such thoughts can grow to become serious self-punishment.

When faced with loss, people naturally feel sad because a person or situation they cared about is gone. Such normal mourning generally lasts for weeks or perhaps months. Loss does not have to involve an extended period of crippling self-punishment. When you discard your defenses and confront your buried feelings, you are freed from a variety of emotional pitfalls. Ideally what emerges at the end of the mourning period is a balanced view of the relationship or situation, with good memories that you can carry with you wherever you go.

Typical defenses we use when faced with a loss are intellectualization, rationalization, helplessness, and anger.

Intellectualization

When we suffer a loss, we may turn to platitudes in an attempt to minimize our pain. When someone dies: "He's gone to a better place" or "It's the best thing." When your kids leave home: "It's time for them to leave the nest." When you lose your life savings: "I've learned a good lesson here."

Although there can be a degree of validity to some intellectualizations, you can't allow them to cover over the emotions that you must experience when sad things happen. When someone close to you dies, you need to face your sadness, grief, and the attendant anger and guilt, and you have to work through them. After a divorce or another significant change in your life, don't allow intellectualization to replace a critical examination of how your emotions and behavior may have contributed to the event.

When something occurs out of the natural order of things—for example, when a child dies—it's very difficult for a parent to come to a ready resolution. In such cases it's appropriate to go from a psychiatric to a philosophical point of view, in the same way that incontrovertible wrongdoing is best addressed through a philosophical approach.

Yet intellectualization has gone too far when it blocks our emotions and our awareness of them. If you can't get used to the fact that your kids have left home or that you have retired from working, spouting conventional wisdom isn't going to help. You have to look beneath this defensive level to what is really bothering you.

Rationalization

When a loss involves the breakup of a relationship, people often rationalize about why the mate left. It's easy to blame the other party, but it's dangerous to rationalize that it's entirely the other person's fault. You should look at your contribution to the separation, because ideally you will go on to another relationship. Even if the things about yourself that you're unhappy about didn't directly lead to the break-up, this is still a good time to look at yourself honestly and directly. The same principle holds true if you are struggling with a reversal of fortunes—for example, when you've lost your job or a lot of money.

Helplessness

Many people adopt the defense of helplessness to cover feelings of rejection and abandonment: "She left me. Poor me, I have nobody. What will happen to me?"

Helplessness is not a state of being. It's an excuse not to take action. There is a comfort in helplessness; it may seem to liberate you from responsibility, but you are not really free. What's more, you are the only one who can overcome your tendency to use this defense. The typical first reaction to this suggestion is irritation and anger at having the burden shifted onto you, the "helpless" one. After all, it is easier to put the onus on others.

However, once you put aside your irritation and acknowledge that helplessness is a defense, you can deal with the emotion that emerges. You may find that you have to confront a picture of yourself as an angry, victimlike, complaining, and self-punishing person. This may not be a pretty picture, but you need to acknowledge it and to experience the pain of that acknowledgment before you can put it behind you.

Anger

After a loss, you may harbor unexpressed anger as a defense against your pain. If somebody leaves you, the anger comes from the blow to your ego, your self-esteem. You're not worthy; your partner prefers somebody else and maybe would rather be alone than with you.

When someone dies, you feel a different kind of anger—the anger of being abandoned. People who are left behind can actually become angry at those who have died. Inside, a voice says, "Look how you've been cheated. You had a great life, but now all that's going to change." Sometimes, if you cry a lot after a loss, you are really shedding tears of anger. If you experience a prolonged period of mourning with excessive crying and misery, you are most likely crying for yourself and not for the person who is gone. The anger gives rise to guilt; you feel guilt about having what you perceive as an inappropriate response when someone you love has died. You weep in an effort to cover your anger and your guilt.

It hurts to say good-bye. After a loss, your life will never be exactly the same; sadness and depression are appropriate and normal for a period of time, in the same way that anger is appropriate when you are threatened or attacked. Everyone is afraid of the unknown and of change, which is the most common occurrence in the human condition.

Loss causes change and raises questions that aren't easily answered. When someone close to you dies, how are you going to manage without that person? Many people can't tolerate being alone. It causes a great deal of panic. When someone leaves you, what are you going to do? You have to leave your job and get a new one. Will it be as good? Will there be as much potential for advancement? What does the future hold for you?

If you don't have anxieties about such matters, there's something wrong. Appropriate levels of anxiety lead to the kind of motivation you need to stay active and vital and to continue evolving. Self-satisfied people stagnate. It's the intensity of your feelings and their duration that you have to question. Too much anxiety is paralyzing.

If you have a good relationship with someone and that person dies, you still have memories that you can carry forward. You can take a part of that person wherever you go, and you can try to incorporate the best aspects of his personality and good works into your own life. We take our happy memories of people with us by emulating their attitudes and behavior. We separate. A part of me goes with you wherever you go, and a part of you goes with me wherever I go. A husband dies and his wife has pleasant memories of him and of their relationship. She lets those memories enrich her life.

In a healthy process of mourning, you feel pain and acknowledge hurt. You keep the channels open for interaction with other people, and you are increasingly able to see the elements of your life come into balance. The situation has changed, but you have the ability to go on. Life offers relationships and pleasures as well as endless opportunities for you to grow, but only if you can let go.

Exploring Your Defenses

Use the self-exploration that follows to help you examine your defenses. This exercise cannot take the place of the dynamic give-and-take of therapy, but it is designed to mirror the process a patient might experience in a short-term therapy session.

Choose a defense that you use frequently. Write down the words you would use to express it. Keep the phrase or sentence in front of you as you ask yourself the following questions in sequence. Record your responses.

As you answer the questions, try to be spontaneous. Above all, be honest with yourself.

1. *Frequency:* Do you often make this statement or one like it? How many times during a typical day or week?
2. *Setting:* What kind of situations are you in when you use this defense?
3. *Irritation level:* If someone suggests that you don't need to feel this way or that what you're saying is not true, do you feel irritated? Are you a little annoyed, but not enough to show it? Annoyed enough to make you lose your train of thought or to change your facial expression? Angry enough to make a remark in response? Angry enough to accuse the other person of not knowing what he or she is talking about? Angry enough to get into a serious quarrel with the other person? The more irritated you feel, the stronger the defense is.
4. *Effect on your life:* How does this belief or feeling affect your behavior and decisions? Are there ways in which it colors your relationship with family, friends, or co-workers? What are those ways?
5. *Problems:* Name at least three problems this defense causes for you—for example, things it prevents you from doing,

or things you do that you know are harmful in some way.

6. *Benefits of dropping the defense:* How would your potential for satisfaction and success be improved if you stopped feeling this way? If you were prevented from using this defense, how would your behavior change with the key people in your life? How would you change the way you spend your time when you are alone? What would you do differently? What would you not do? Imagine what your life would be like today, over the next week, the next month. How could your life change over the course of a year?

7. *What lies beneath this defense?* What are you hiding from in using this defense? When you first began using it, what was going on in your life? What was your strongest feeling at that time? Was it anger? Guilt? Pain or hurt?

8. *Be specific about the underlying feeling.* (A similar exercise, entitled "Exploring Your Hidden Feelings," follows Chapter 9.)

Keep the record you have made of this defense. After a few days, go over the questions and your responses. Doing the exercise for the first time increases your awareness. When you think about the defense a second time, you may gain a fuller understanding of how it operates in your life.

An excellent way to get even greater benefit from this exercise is to review it with someone who knows you well. Invite a friend whom you trust to review your responses with you. Insist that your friend be completely honest with you. When working through the questions with another person, you very likely will be able to elaborate on items 1 through 6, and, depending on how well your friend knows you, you may come to further insights about items 7 and 8.

This self-exploration has been designed for repeated

use with various defenses. Resistance to facing painful feelings does not go away quickly or easily. But your continued efforts will pay off as you become increasingly willing to discard the defenses that stand in the way of self-awareness.

CHAPTER 9

Learning to Live without Defenses

A stranger approached an old man on the outskirts of a town and asked what kind of people lived there. Before answering, the old man questioned the stranger about the people who lived in the village he came from. He replied, "They were malicious, dishonest, and mean."

"Well," said the old man, "those are the kinds of people you will find here."

A short while later another stranger came to town and asked the same question. When the old man inquired about the people the second stranger had left behind, he replied, "They were good people, honest and hardworking."

The old man told him, "Those are the kinds of people you will find here."

This old man understood a truth about human nature— that the way people perceive the world and how the world responds to them may be determined by a factor that is beyond their awareness.

Intrinsic in short-term therapy's technique is the appeal to the individual to take action. How to change? The answer is part and parcel of the therapy's technique: the challenge to the defenses and the focus on your buried feelings exhort you to go from a passive to an active stance, to take charge of the way you look at life and deal with your emotions.

There is only one way to accomplish emotional change. After you've reassessed your perceptions and clarified your feelings by taking an inventory, you have to ask yourself this question: "What am I going to do about my problems?" Not what is your therapist going to do about them, or your boss, your wife, or your friends. Self-help books, like therapy, can help clarify the issues that are most important to you. But in the end you're the one who has to strap on the six-gun and go out on the dirt road. No one else can do it for you.

Rescue fantasies are as old as mankind, as is magical thinking, the belief that things will go your way without any action on your part. But there is no shortcut to emotional change. Short-term therapy, in its philosophy and its technique, is a call to action.

Magical Thinking Won't Work

Magical thinking is believing that something will happen without any meaningful effort on your part. For instance, as a delivery boy approaches a beautiful house, he has a fantasy that a gorgeous girl will open the door and her father will be a multimillionaire. The girl will fall in love with him and marry him, and her father will take him into his company and make him a vice president. He will become chairman of the board when his father-in-law retires. This fantasy lacks one important element: preparation for that role in life.

The lack of meaningful action characterizes all magical thinking. Frequently we hear people say, "If it's meant to be,

I'll get that new job" or "Everything will work out for the best." Such sentiments are ways of staying put. They allow people to avoid taking the action that is needed to effect change.

Magical thinking can be a fantasy or it can be a point of view, but it always involves either a shortcut or the replacement of one task with another that is less effective. A wife who feels unloved may think that if she does an excellent job of ironing her husband's shirts he will treat her with more affection. However, ironing, cooking, and cleaning are not meaningful substitutes for intimacy. In this type of magical thinking, we cast ourselves in a role in order to avoid looking at some of the realistic ingredients that go into making our lives work.

In childhood, magical thinking is normal. Children believe that time is infinite, that they will live forever, and therefore that all things are possible. Everything they want will come to them sooner or later. By contrast, in the reality of a finite, or adult, sense of time, not all things are possible. In an adult reality, decisions and choices become much more significant, as does a sense of how we expend our psychic energy and how we get in our own way.

When you're in the thrall of emotions and impulses you aren't facing, you tend to indulge in magical thinking. You think that time is infinite, that you don't have to do anything to bring about change, that things will take care of themselves. Magical thinking is a way of viewing the future while still using your defenses.

Tolerating Your Anxiety

You must train yourself to mistrust the negative feelings and impulses generated when you look past your defenses to uncomfortable or painful memories. The process of clarifying those memories, emotions, and the impulses they elicit generates anxiety; your fantasies about those impulses make you anxious. Anxiety—a sense of unrest, tension, and heightened feelings unrelated to any immediate reality—is part of the human condition. It's not unique to any group of people; it happens to all of us at some point in our lives.

If you believe that you didn't do all you might have done for your father before he died, you may attempt to avoid that painful thought. If you look at it, you're going to feel some anxiety as you take inventory of all your emotions. You may feel an impulse to self-sabotage based on guilt feelings that arise. But only by tolerating that anxiety will you be able to scrutinize your feelings and deal with them in a way that will be productive for you.

When the anxiety implicit in this scrutiny presents itself, you can do one of two things. You can deal with it by moving away from the memory and the emotion—burying it once again, utilizing defenses, banishing the thought, turning away from the confrontation—and thereby temporarily lessening the anxiety you feel. Or you can identify that anxiety as a natural component of the process of reevaluating and bringing to the surface those memories, emotions, and impulses.

Identifying your anxiety will lead to the clarity you need to put your problem issues in perspective; it will allow for a diminution of their impact and for the opportunity to rechannel your emotional resources to new, productive areas. If, on the other hand, you banish the painful thoughts that arise, then the modes of behavior, the patterns of thinking, and the defenses that you use to cover those memories and emotions will continue. Like the tide, they will return, impeding your progress toward emotional change and self-awareness.

Continued avoidance will cause your anxiety to loom large and take on a life of its own; it will become in itself a force to be defended against. Now you're really handicapped. You not only have painful feelings and memories;

you also fear the onset of the anxiety. If you are committed to a process of change, you must become comfortable with the knowledge that anxiety is going to be generated. You must understand that, just like painful emotions and impulses, anxiety is normal and can be dealt with. Avoiding anxiety heightens its overwhelming and debilitating quality.

It's similar to building or toning muscles. When you're lifting a weight and you feel tired, the natural impulse is to put it down. But in order to strengthen your muscles you have to push past that feeling of tiredness to the point of muscle failure. If you're not willing to tolerate that discomfort, you're not going to derive any significant benefit from the exercise.

Likewise, if you're not willing to push your important emotional issues past the point of your anxieties about them, then you're going to avoid them. You're going to put that mental barbell down before the point of improvement.

As you become better equipped to live with the initial discomfort of being emotionally self-aware, the conflicts and problems of your life become attenuated. They never go away completely, but you feel relief and an easing of the pain they once caused you. As your comfort in confronting issues becomes greater, the balance tips toward a life lived with positive emotions, with attitudes and types of behavior that work in your favor rather than against you.

Feeling Your Anger

Some people have trouble feeling their anger because they fear what they will do. They think that once they let out a little anger, the floodgates will open. Others have trouble expressing anger in an appropriate way. Consider, for example, a man who is cut off as he drives on the highway: he speeds after the offending car, honking his horn, screaming out the window, and cutting the other driver off in turn—not a productive way to demonstrate anger. When you feel anger, it's inappropriate to stifle the emotion, to displace it (kick the dog, throw things), to fantasize about your rage, to weep, or to leave the room.

The key to feeling your anger is realizing that what is frightening about it is often your belief in your fantasies. For instance, you're passed over for a promotion you believe you deserve. For years you've worked hard, received outstanding performance reviews, and produced excellent results for the company, but the boss plays tennis with the person who got the position. Faced with this injustice, your fantasy might be to throw your boss out the window.

The problem is that one part of your psyche registers that fantasy as if it were reality. Over the course of their lives people build up repertories of "homicidal" actions that they try to repress or flee from, frequently by taking a passive stance in an attempt to counterbalance, defuse, subdue, and ignore their rage. If you've dealt with anger in the past by going into a rage or by having fantasies of maiming or killing, when a provocative situation occurs you may not deal with the anger of the moment; instead of expressing it in an appropriate way, you may deal with your perception of what the anger is to you—homicidal or an all-encompassing and engulfing rage, a lashing out and a loss of control. Because of your perception, you may cover your anger with defenses.

Charles, for example, became a passive, frozen, paralyzed man, unable to tolerate anything that seemed the least bit confrontational, because his anger was overwhelming to him. When he was growing up, he had repeated rageful homicidal fantasies about his stepfather, and those fantasies nearly came to fruition in one dramatic episode.

Afterward Charles lived with the belief that he was a potential if not an actual murderer. If someone cut in front of him in the grocery store line, he couldn't say anything for fear he would lose control, rip the person's head off, and throw it down the aisle with the bananas and the vegetables. If you asked him, "Why didn't you say anything?" he'd answer, "I didn't want to cause a disturbance" or "They might have thrown me out of the store" or "The person might have had a gun." But that's not really what he was concerned about; he was anxious about his own rage breaking loose.

There's only one productive way to deal with your anger, and that is to declare it in an appropriate way. But in order to express it, you first have to be comfortable with it. When you feel angry, you may indulge in violent fantasies to make yourself feel better, or you may vent your rage internally in a very dramatic fashion. If so, a part of you will view yourself as an out-of-control maniac, and it's going to be difficult for you to look somebody in the eye and say, "The way you treated me makes me angry. I want something different from you."

It's not easy to make this simple statement if you see yourself as a part-time ax murderer, or if you've habitually dealt with anger by screaming and shouting, throwing things, lashing out at people, driving your car at high speeds, breaking objects, crying, avoiding situations or leaving the room. People who behave that way—in reality or in their fantasies—have an exaggerated view of what their anger is about, and it's frightening.

What role should anger play in your life? It should prompt you to scrutinize perceived attacks and carefully consider the response that will be in your best interest. Do you want to lose yourself in fantasies about killing the boss? Do you want to get headaches or ulcers, go home and yell at your kids and fight with your mate? Those are all ways to channel and deal with anger, but none of them will help you.

You always have options, some more viable than others. If you're passed over for promotion, one option is to get another job. If you can't find a satisfactory position, you may be stuck where you are. But the fact is that your choices are often not as limited as you may think. Frequently the sensation of being stuck is a rationalization for not taking charge of your life.

There are times, though, when realistically it's just not possible or wise to change jobs. In that case, ideally you should be able to go to your boss and make some statement on your behalf, not because it's going to get you the promotion but because you're going to feel that within your world you're dealing with events appropriately—you're not displacing your responses and you're not taking them out on yourself.

Try not to misperceive your anger. Examine your perception of your anger, especially if you perceive it as a potentially violent explosion. Then strive to judge the appropriateness of the anger and to express it in the way that best serves you. Over time, this kind of scrutiny will help you feel comfortable when you need to express anger.

Making an appropriate response means learning to communicate your angry feelings. You may think that you have two choices: no response or a nuclear response. You may not see a middle ground, and you may instead live in the extremes of silence, using avoidance or rationalization, having visions of expressing your anger violently, turning the applecart over, blowing the top off of situations.

There are appropriate ways to communicate this strong emotion. Believe it or not, "I am angry with you" is an effective statement of anger. It says that you are experiencing—viscerally, intellectually, and emotionally—a set of sensations that are upsetting. Reporting on those sensations is an appropriate way to demonstrate anger, and other people will usually accept what you have to say. Expressing feelings means that dialogue and mutual understanding become possible.

Showing your anger to others may not always be in the service of being open, honest, and intimate. If it doesn't result in a resolution, it can be a distancing mechanism designed to maintain the walls of the defenses. Striving for a resolution to your anger is essential. Unresolved anger is like high cholesterol or carrying extra weight: it isn't good for you.

Coping with Pain and Hurt

Like everyone else, you will experience pain and hurt. It's the intensity of those feelings, their duration, and what you do about them that's important. If you choose to live with chronic pain and hurt, then you're going to live like a victim—feeling that you were cheated, that you did not get what you needed out of life because others deprived you of it. But there are other ways to respond.

When you say good-bye to people or situations, you feel a justifiable sadness or even grief. It's all right to acknowledge that disappointment and rejection hurt. It's appropriate to acknowledge your sadness and pain and sorrow. The problem occurs when that pain continues for a prolonged period.

If you temporarily feel hurt because you were stood up by a date, that's appropriate. The human ego is not bulletproof. It is vulnerable. But you should not treat your ego as if it were made of fine china. People who view their psyches as extremely fragile become chronic victims, feeding on the notion that they have been cheated and that pain and hurt are their lot in life.

Dostoyevski observed that man seeks suffering as an end, but he was speaking in larger, more philosophical terms. We are talking about something that is more mundane and petty—the seeking of pain and hurt and the manipulation of our environment by using those feelings in the service of self-victimization. Pain and hurt, if harbored and cherished, can give rise to the crippling defense of helplessness.

As an end in itself, the continued ventilation of hurt and pain only leads to chronic anger and bitterness, which, no matter how justified, is not productive. When feelings of hurt and pain are not resolved, when the person who has been hurt cannot move on, the victimizer ends up having as much control as a punitive parent might over the victim's life.

Fighting the effects of chronic pain and hurt requires basically the same effort that you must make in dealing with any unproductive, draining, maladaptive attitude or behavior. You must look very frankly at yourself, tolerating the worst things about yourself, the things you really don't want to see, the things that cause you guilt and pain, that you've attempted to ignore or avoid or hide. It's easy to recount what others did to you, but it's very difficult to admit to yourself what you did to them. You might find it easy to think that your mother cheated you, yet it's very difficult for you to accept the idea that you cheated your mother.

Evaluate your perception of what was done to you. Then ask yourself some questions: What did I do to the person who hurt me? What was my contribution, if any, to this person's reaction to me? Maybe you won't find anything, but you have to take a look. More often than not, a critical self-examination will provide you with more than a one-dimensional view of how you've been treated. You're likely to find that you've participated in your own perceived victimization.

Let's say you've come across one of the times in your life when you actually have been victimized. As discussed in Chapter 4, being hurt carries with it the implication that you deserve to be hurt. It can lead to an impulse on your part to accept or to exaggerate this implication. Devaluation heightens the hurt and brings to it a sense of sadness, victimization, and at times, anger.

When you recall experiencing a significant hurt—a loss, a criticism, a rejection—make an inventory of the emotions that accompanied your pain. Cataloging the variety of feelings and attitudes that the experience produced, in the same way that you would enumerate all of the emotions that might exist along with anger, will dissipate the impulse to exaggerate the sense of devaluation stimulated by being hurt. Taking an inventory of your emotions will allow you to experience your hurt within a realistic context—one that is limited to the circumstances surrounding the loss, the criticism, the rejection—rather than to see it as a larger-than-life statement about who and what you are.

Now you have to ask yourself some hard questions. You feel victimized, and you've been going through life with your shoulders stooped, head bowed, bemoaning your fate. Why do you want to keep doing that to yourself? You've taken what somebody else did to you and incorporated it into how you view yourself. You are perpetuating your own self-punishment. You are allowing yourself to be an emotional hostage to the person or persons who mistreated you. You owe yourself more than that. What is it within you that insists that you behave this way? And what are you going to do about it?

The question—what are you going to do about it? —suggests going from a passive to an active posture. That's what therapists try to do and what I've been urging continuously in this book. The answer to the question is that you're going to take charge of your life.

The first time I ask a patient, "What do you want to do about your problems?" the patient usually feels irritated and annoyed because I'm not providing the answer. People in a passive mode do not like to be asked to think about themselves in an active way. But you are the only person who can take the actions that are required for the working through of your emotional problems.

There is no shortcut, pill, or magical phrase that you can substitute for action. You are the only person who can make the willful decision to change. It cannot be made by the author of a book or a therapist or a well-intentioned friend or relative.

Will Medication Help?

People who suffer from severe and chronic depression may not be able to use therapy alone to clarify and resolve their oppressive feelings. In these cases the therapist and patient should consider whether medication could help. Many people have derived enormous benefit from proper medication for depression. There are times when short-term therapy is best used in conjunction with medication.

Unfortunately some people still believe that medications that affect the feelings are only for crazy people. This misperception prevents many people from using antidepressive medication that could alleviate their suffering effectively and rapidly.

Facing Your Guilty Feelings

Ruminating about making mistakes and doing the wrong thing is a form of self-flagellation. It should not be confused with confronting feelings of guilt, clearing away misperceptions, and striving for a resolution that allows you to move forward.

The only way you can clarify feelings of guilt is to face the painful central issue: What is it that you feel guilty about? When examined closely, the charge of guilt often cannot be upheld.

"If I had treated my wife better, she wouldn't have left" or "If I had stayed home that night, my husband wouldn't have died." Sometimes such feelings are simply not valid. The wife might have left for someone else anyway, and the husband's poor health is what caused him to die. But as long as the perception remains, so does the guilt. We must look at our guilty feelings and determine their validity.

One type of guilt arises as a sense of wrongdoing by association and is based on misperception. You perceive your mother as having struggled hard; she did everything she could to help you while leading a joyless life, denying herself any happiness. From such a perception it's a short jump to the belief that you were a parasite. You did not carry your load; she did all, you did nothing. However, it's easy to forget that each of us—including every significant person in our lives—has a past that makes us who we are. According to our needs, we determine how we are going to operate in the world in relation to the people around us. This type of guilt by association is inappropriate. If you look at your guilt, you may come to the conclusion that everything wasn't the way you perceived it to be. You may gain satisfaction from a renewed sense of emotional balance.

However, some guilt is based on reality. A patient tells me: "My mother was dying in the hospital. I knew she was very sick, but I couldn't deal with it and spent the weekend in Las Vegas. My mother died alone, without the comfort of anyone she knew. I did a terrible thing by cheating her of the kind of death she wanted." In many ways, this is an enlightened statement. This man is aware that he was not able to deal with his mother's death. But that reality does not help the way he feels. He suffers from guilt because he let his mother down; he was not there for her when he might have been and could have been. And his guilt is valid. He did wrong.

One inappropriate way to deal with wrongdoing is to ritualize it. In films depicting organized crime, how do the gangsters make it right in their minds when they routinely murder people? They've built an elaborate mechanism and code surrounding murder—how it's done, where it's done, who gives permission for it, and who actually kills the person. They're so focused on the ritualistic behavior that surrounds the killings—the rationale for them and the details of how they will be done—that they don't have to think about what they're doing. Because they ritualize so elaborately, these criminals are psychopaths, people who lack a consciousness of the moral implications of their actions. Their ritualization is a complex form of rationalization.

The nonpsychopath, the man who didn't go to his mother when she was dying, may likewise try to rationalize why he didn't do the right thing. Some types of therapy would try to help him deal with guilt by rationalizing it away: "Everybody acts that way. How were you to know that she was going to die that day?" He did know. That can't be glossed over. "Your mom understood. You had a reduced-rate fare, and she didn't want you to spend the extra money to get back from Vegas." Such wrong-headed supportive talk is not going to help this man deal with his guilt. He did the wrong thing. The therapist must help him assume responsibility for his actions.

Dismissing what you did, rationalizing it away, or burying it in some other way is not going to help; you're going to suffer unless you resolve your guilt. Otherwise it is going to undermine, to a greater or a lesser degree, the quality of your life and what you can contribute to the lives of those around you. When you have cheated someone close to you, must you go forward and cheat others, including yourself? That does not enhance the quality of life on this planet. You have to develop the ability to forgive yourself.

What can the man who didn't go to his dying mother's bedside do about his guilt? Will it cause him to emulate his mother as he perceived her? Will he live so that he will end the same way, a miserable human being dying an isolated death because that's what he caused for her? Must he suffer for the rest of his life?

All of us have done wrong. However you think of wrongdoing—as missing the mark or as sinning—it is a condition of existence. You cannot proceed through life flawlessly, without imperfection. There have been times when you could have made a different choice or done more, but you didn't. The reason doesn't matter. The reality is that your actions fell short of what you consider appropriate. If you allow yourself to be handicapped and to suffer endlessly with that burden, then you as an individual and the human race in general are only going to head in the wrong direction.

If you do not reassess your guilt, you run the risk of repeating your wrongful actions in your relationships in the present and the future. Because you have cheated people in the past, you may cheat others in the future because of the insidious thought that you are not entitled to their nourishment, intimacy, goodwill. In other words, guilt can lead to a sense of lack of entitlement: I did not give and therefore I am not worthy to receive.

It takes a great deal of strength and resolution to come back from committing a wrong. Resolution of this type of guilt begins with the ability to acknowledge "That's the way it was. I did wrong."

Living with Your Failures

When you really have done wrong and are willing to face it, what can you do? How can you deal with being flawed? How do you compensate for your imperfections? Because psychotherapy cannot provide answers to these questions, the response must become a philosophical rather than a psychiatric one.

In our attempts to offset our failures—our wrongdoings, the effects of our misperceptions, the emotional suffering we have inflicted on ourselves and others—we are seeking, in essence, a definition of the concept of virtue. Plato said, "Knowledge is Virtue." Over the centuries, people have debated what he meant by that comment. Did he mean that to know is virtuous? Or did he mean that knowledge is synonymous with virtue? And what is the knowledge that we are trying to obtain?

Is it to know everything that is in an encyclopedia, to know how to paint, how to write, how to repair a car? Is it to know how to be a doctor, a lawyer, an accountant? The ancients' definition of virtue was hitting the mark, doing what you can do to the best of your ability. That narrow definition provides us with a specific interpretation of virtue in terms of what we do in our careers and relationships, how we perform in our everyday lives.

However, if we expand the concept of virtue to its broadest extent, what does it mean? An expanded definition of virtue must make a statement about our ultimate goal on this planet. In this global sense, virtue is to know, to understand, what the proper function of humanity should be and to live in a way that furthers that goal.

Plato again addressed this issue in the *Apology*, which presents the defense of Socrates when he was on trial in Athens. In spite of the stated charges, Socrates understands that he has been condemned to death because he is a gadfly, provoking people to think. Indeed, he says to his judges after the sentence has been passed, "And if I were to say to you that to discourse daily about Virtue is the greatest good and that the unexamined life is not worth living, you would not believe me anyway."

Plato understood that man has difficulty devising a prescription that works against his impulse to look no further than his own needs. When he discusses virtue, to my mind he is speaking of that greater good, which is to serve others, as Socrates did; indeed, Socrates gave up his life for the greater good by attempting to be a gadfly to his society.

There is a way, a prescription for relating to one another that will increase the quantity and the quality of good in the universe, and that is service to others.

Service to others doesn't necessarily entail enormous

self-sacrifice or numerous charitable acts. It does require caring and respect for the circumstances of other people. It means being considerate of the people around you and trying to help them in any way you can. It means easing their pain and suffering, facilitating their lives whenever possible. The pioneering chemist Louis Pasteur put it succinctly when he said, "If I can carry one stone to the pillars of truth, I will have accomplished something." If you decide that you have a debt to the past, then service to others is a way to repay it.

In pondering the ultimate question of why we exist, we may not be able to give a demonstrable answer. But we can make the case, based on human history and centuries of dialogue, that our goal should be to lead the most satisfying existence we can. Service to others is the only reliable path to that satisfaction. Deviating from that path leads us away from satisfaction to conflict and dissension and a diminution of what is good in the world.

You will never be able to avoid doing wrong, because perfection doesn't exist in the human state. Part of forgiving yourself is understanding that doing wrong is inherent in existence. But forgiving yourself need not be just a mental attitude. You can pay on the debt you owe to other people, to the past, to humanity in general. You can make up for your wrongdoing by trying to stress the positive, by doing right, by serving others. And that service will also benefit you.

Once in conversation I stated my belief that service to others is the greatest good. "Good for others" was one person's reply. No, good for me. Like everyone else, I live my life according to the theory of expectancy: how I behave toward others is what I expect from them in return. If I am helpful and considerate, I live with a comfortable sense of my neighbors. If I cheat, steal, or do evil, I am uncomfortable because I expect to be repaid in kind. This theory explains why criminals have no sense of trust and are paranoid about other people. What they are capable of inflicting on others they believe others are capable of inflicting on them. So my behavior can be its own reward or punishment.

I saw a television news story about a psychiatrist who worked in a center for terminally ill children. One little boy was complaining about his circumstances, and the psychiatrist said to him, "The problem is that you're not being useful to anyone." At first, this seems an outrageous and unduly harsh statement to make to a dying child. But, if understood within the context of what human life is about, it makes sense. Service to others, or usefulness (a term that I also associate with the concept of intimacy), provides nourishment to the spirit. The psychiatrist was trying to help the child experience a sense of well-being during the final months of his life. In response to the psychiatrist's suggestion, the boy began to correspond with a child in another state who also suffered with a terminal disease. In their letters and phone calls, the two discussed, among other topics, their worst fears and their emotional ups and downs as their illnesses were treated.

Your obligations to others, to yourself, and to society as a whole are inextricably linked. You owe yourself and the people around you more than to indulge in punishing self-sabotage. Rather than indulging in self-defeating attitudes and behavior, you can say, "That's the way it was," but with an eye to the future, with a resolve that you're going to go on in life and, in an extended sense, redress your failures. This concept, whether intuited or explicitly embraced, is what allows doctors to keep going when a patient dies, especially when they have inadvertently contributed to that death.

In our society, physicians are rewarded materially and accorded respect because they live with their failures. They are not rewarded because they know how to do something that others can't do or because they've taken a great deal of time to learn their trade or because they save lives. Physicians receive compensation for dying a little bit with each patient who dies.

There is no physician who has not made a mistake and contributed to somebody's death. The doctor, like the person who let his dying mother down, has to live with mistakes. If doctors were to internalize their failures as guilt and go on to sabotage themselves, they would cheat their other patients, and the quality of medicine would be in dire straits.

I was a fourth-year medical student when I faced that situation for the first time. A woman with a serious cardiac problem was being considered for surgery to correct a gastrointestinal condition. After discussion about whether the preliminary procedures and surgery would compromise her heart, tests were ordered that involved inserting a tube through her nose, down her throat, and into her stomach. As I was sitting by her bedside suctioning out her gastric juices for analysis, the patient complained of pressure in her chest.

I reported this to the intern on duty, who attributed the pressure to the presence of the tube. I went back to the bedside, and all of a sudden the woman's eyes rolled back and she passed out. We called for help and the resuscitation team arrived. The assistant chief resident said to me, "Why don't you go upstairs to the coffee shop?" because he realized that I was upset by what was happening. I didn't go.

We rushed the patient to the treatment room. The doctors pumped on her heart, but the monitor showed a flat line. At that point, I saw her son—a boy of about ten—arrive for visiting hours. I could see him through the glass window of the room, but he couldn't see in. The thoracic surgeon took the scalpel, opened the woman's chest, and started massaging her heart, and I knew it was all over.

One of the residents sat down on a bench next to the

boy and talked to him. After a few minutes the boy left. As I watched him walk out of the hospital, I remembered myself as a child. When I was eight years old, my father had had his first coronary, and I spent the next seventeen years waiting for him to die. When this patient died five years after my father did, her little boy's irrevocable loss had a meaning for me that was personal.

Faced with that patient's death, what were my options? There is always the initial thought, which is the epitome of guilt: "I should leave this place. I'm not suited, I'm not qualified." Should I have left medicine and gone into advertising? Punished myself by turning to drink or drugs? Or tried to take what I had learned and help the next person who came through the door? I chose to stay.

But even as I help the next person and promote the idea that service to others is the greatest good, do I believe that I am totally off the hook? Can I ever forget what happened in that case and in the three or four others in which I believed I contributed to a patient's death? No. I will carry that with me. It would be better if it had never happened, but that's not the way it was. I will never completely lose the sense of having let those people down, but the feelings become attenuated as I work with others.

This important issue is not dealt with in medical school or in the residency training of physicians, and I believe that many of my colleagues have died because they never resolved it. They burned out or had coronaries because they couldn't live with their failures. Medicine—the living and the dying of it—overtook them; they fell prey to its pressures because they didn't have a philosophical sextant to guide them through the storm.

This issue is not unique to the practice of medicine. In the same way that physicians have to carry the burden of their mistakes and make something productive of them, all people face the challenge of living with their failures, sometimes in a dramatic way, sometimes in a mundane way, but always in a painful way. Guilt, whether it stems from terrible errors or from everyday shortcomings, is universal. However, you can turn it around and increase your usefulness to other people. You don't get off the hook, but from your experiences—good and bad—you can alter what you do and think in the future.

Putting Your Feelings in Balance

Attempting to understand the everyday issues that complicate your life—remaining open-minded and critical about them—helps you have an appropriate awareness of and response to emotional events that are potentially devastating. It helps you see people realistically, rather than have your perceptions colored by unresolved emotional interactions.

Are you able to acknowledge good feelings about a person you associate with a distressing time or event? If not, you don't have a realistic and balanced view of your relationship with that person. There are no people in our lives whom we can realistically view in absolute terms. Considerable unnecessary anger, guilt, and pain result from not appreciating that there are both positive and negative aspects within all intimate relationships.

The conversation that follows shows the way I dealt with someone who was married to the notion that he had only one feeling about a certain person. An ambitious young man who was eager to please, Joe saw himself as always giving 110 percent to any task. During one session, he complained about his boss:

Joe: The head of my department decided that I shouldn't go to the seminar.
Zois: How does that make you feel?
Joe: I hate him. I'm very angry at him. He's really a terrible person.

Zois: Have you ever thought of him not being here?
Joe: Do you mean dead?
Zois: That word comes to your mind.
Joe: Yes, I have. When he makes me angry I picture him getting killed in a car accident.
Zois: Can you visualize him in that car accident?
Joe: No, I never have.
Zois: Can you do it now?
Joe: Well, that sounds pointless.
Zois: You have some difficulty with this. You say it's pointless, so you rationalize. Can you look at it?

Joe could not appropriately declare his anger because he took it to an extreme in his mind. He linked his anger with the thought of his boss being dead. That thought provided fertile soil for guilt and conflicted feelings. By getting Joe to experience his anger and see it clearly, I reduced his anxiety about it and allowed him to view it within the context of his other emotions.

Joe: It would be terrible. He would be still, covered with blood.
Zois: How do you feel as you look at it?
Joe: I feel uncomfortable.
Zois: What's the emotion?
Joe: I feel bad.

At this point I began to accomplish the transition from Joe's angry feelings to his tender feelings. Joe can now start to make an inventory of the complex set of emotions engendered by his relationship with his boss.

Zois: What would you miss about your boss if he died?
Joe: Well, he had a certain way of helping me out with projects when I was stuck, and one time when things had gone very well he took me to lunch, and

we were talking about the kinds of music we liked.
I would miss those things about him.

Zois: You have a lot of mixed feelings about your boss.

Joe: Yes, I do.

Zois: So when you say you hate him in relation to not
allowing you to go to the seminar, in fact there
are a lot of feelings under that hate, a lot of painful
and positive feelings.

Joe: Yes, I never looked at it that way, but I can see that
now.

In order to get Joe to experience his emotions fully, I
elicit details about his thoughts. At first, some of the questions may seem irrelevant or picky, but they are specifically
designed to stimulate expression of all the emotions that Joe
may have for his boss. Minute description is important in
bringing feelings to the surface so that patient and therapist
can subject them to scrutiny.

In Chapter 1, Charles provided a similar, though
more dramatic, example of a person who saw only one
side of a complicated relationship, and in other chapters
we saw how patients who were isolated and locked into the
angry victim role moved from a one-sided view in which
intimacy was not possible to an awareness that they also
had tender feelings and that pleasant emotions also existed
in their relationships.

Many therapists, with all the best intentions, make the
mistake of siding with their patients against people with
whom the patients have problems. When patients talk about
their pain and suffering, it's not surprising that the therapist cares about them and empathizes with their pain. But
that caring can be therapeutically ineffectual if the therapist
then takes on the role of protector rather than clarifier.

The pointlessness of a therapist siding with patients
is brought into focus when we consider a hypothetical
situation: The patient's spouse is also in therapy with

another practitioner who empathizes with his or her suffering. In effect, each supportive therapist supports his own patient's view of the other person. As William James queried in *The Varieties of Religious Experience*, when faced with conflicting irrationalities, which do we choose? The therapist who sides with the patient feeds into the patient's sense of being victimized and cheated. Having a cheerleader for a therapist, encouraging you as you carry the ball down the field, may be okay for a period of time, but it's not curative. It doesn't enable you to free yourself from the conflicts that burden you.

Many patients tell me that they have had a very unhappy relationship with one of their parents. When I ask them what they miss or might miss about their mother or father, they insist they can think of nothing. Only under a great deal of pressure from me do they acknowledge certain happy memories, and even then they usually minimize them. That's not real life. One feeling is always associated with a converse feeling. That's what all relationships are about. The key to dealing with a negative or troubling emotional response is to do an inventory of all the emotions associated with an event or a situation rather than to focus only on the prevalent one while ignoring the rest.

One way I establish that a balance of feelings exists within a relationship is to ask: "What would you miss about your father if he were to die?" Another is to establish the hypothesis that the patient had died instead; I then ask what the person in question would miss about him or her. The response often gives rise to a more rounded and balanced view of a relationship.

If you say that you associate no positive feelings with a given relationship, you are avoiding some knowledge or awareness—and at great expense to yourself because most likely your perception is not true. It can be difficult to acknowledge that a person who makes you angry is also a person for whom you have tender feelings. It's hard to say,

"Yes, my mother was often short-tempered and harsh with me, but sometimes she was caring and supportive."

Sorting out your mixed emotions and developing a balanced view of your past and present relationships is vitally important in keeping yourself free from the manipulations of your negative feelings. It is essential in preventing anger from dominating your life. If you suffer from intense and chronic rage or if you have taken on the angry victim role, you may be able to resolve your problems by getting in touch with the tender feelings of a relationship and seeing its good side.

Likewise, developing a balanced view of relationships is one of the keys to breaking a cycle of hurt and pain. If you feel victimized, you can look at what your contribution may have been to the hurt and pain that you suffered. Even if you were an innocent victim, you can resist the temptation to view yourself from that time onward as a victim.

You can embrace your hurt and pain, wearing them as a badge of honor or, in a more balanced approach, take action to live a life that is full and whole. One of the most important tasks of the therapist is to assist you in making the transition from the angry victim role to the acknowledgment of tender and caring emotions. Only through this acknowledgment can you clear the path to intimacy.

In a slightly different way, striving for a balanced view will help to alleviate your guilt. If you feel guilty, then tender feelings already exist in abundance—you have an excess of feeling for the person or situation in question. What you need is, first, a balanced perspective in order to evaluate whether your guilt is truly valid; and, second, if the sense of wrongdoing remains, a determination of what kind of repayment you can make for a wrong done in the past. For instance, you might not have been close to your mother at the end of her life, and you may tell yourself that the two of you didn't get along. However, there may have been good elements in the relationship that you have ignored in the service of beating yourself up. And if you feel that you really did let your mother down, life presents many opportunities for atonement in the future.

If you insist that you have only negative feelings about someone in your life, keep searching, because that's not possible. Balance is curative; it opens the door to accomplishing intimacy because it attenuates your negative emotions and makes them manageable.

The Triumph of Living without Defenses

There is a philosophical point of view that says there are no objective statements, only value judgments. Even stating "two plus two equals four" means placing our faith in the concept of mathematics implied in that simple equation. Many philosophers—Plato, Kierkegaard, Nietzsche—have elaborated on the idea that all truth is subjective. When you leave the room, how do you know the room exists? What is the sound of a tree falling in the forest if no one is there to hear it? In terms of the human psyche, this point of view translates to the idea that each person is the author of his or her emotional universe.

Everything you see and sense is colored by your feelings. When your unexamined emotions and impulses are in control, they color your perceptions of your experience. Your task in scrutinizing these feelings is to attain a balanced emotional outlook, one that is productive and conducive to experiencing the world in a positive manner.

When you have worked through your most painful emotional problems, guilt and its offshoot, self-sabotage, will cease to exist in any meaningful way. You will increase your ability to make decisions based on your best interests. Likewise, intense and chronic anger will lessen and stop manifesting itself in a traumatic and devastating fashion, and your aggressive impulses will become more manageable. You will stop playing the angry victim role once you have acknowledged your own contribution to the hurt and pain you have experienced.

Grief will assume an appropriate place on your emotional landscape. You'll feel sad from time to time because people and situations have been lost to you, but the feelings of loss will be balanced by the happy memories you will carry wherever you go.

What will emerge is an increased ability to accomplish intimacy and the richness of an existence based on closeness with others. As your ability to be intimate with other people grows stronger, your chances for a sustained sense of well-being will be greatly enhanced. Restless discontent will diminish and will eventually be replaced by appropriate aspirations, productive planning, and the ability to tolerate frustration in the face of striving—in other words, your energy will be channeled into productive directions.

When you are free of the dictates of your buried feelings, you will develop an emotionally healthy philosophy of life within the context of your own personal world. I'm referring to what used to be called wisdom. A Chinese philosopher described a wise man as one who hears the cock crow in the neighboring village and yet has never traveled there; instead he journeys with his mind. This is someone who is in harmony and at peace with his world, whose life is complete because of his understanding of it.

We can all develop a sense of harmony and peace within our lives. We can look at the world in a more philosophical and more optimistic way. That, after all, is the goal of plumbing the depths of our psyches. We do it so that we can use our intellect and reason to view the world with clarity rather than through a haze of painful emotions, memories, and impulses that color our perceptions and experiences.

Exploring Your Hidden Feelings

Use the following self-exploration to help yourself examine your most difficult emotions. These questions cannot substitute for conversations with a therapist, but they reflect the process of thought and feeling that might take place in a short-term therapy session.

The questions are designed to address the emotions in your life in a systematic way. They cover the main elements of any emotional experience: an event, your memory of that event, the emotion generated by the event and the memory, and the impulse born of that emotion. An inventory takes into account the other emotions that existed around the event.

In responding to the questions, try to be spontaneous, but stay true to your deepest feelings. Above all, be honest with yourself.

Set aside a half hour or more to consider a deep feeling—an underlying problem or emotion that your defenses may be blocking. You might want to think about a problem or an emotion that you identified at the end of the self-exploration at the end of Chapter 8. Write a brief description of your problem or emotion, beginning with the words "I feel..." For example:

- "I feel angry that..."
- "I feel hurt that..."
- "I feel sad that..."
- "I feel guilty that..."

Keep these descriptions in front of you as you undertake the following self-exploration. Make notes if you like.

1. *How do you usually express this feeling?* Do you express it

verbally? Only to yourself, or to other people as well? What words do you use? Do you express it in a nonverbal way? Do you cry? Do you have strong physical sensations such as flushed skin or an increased heartbeat? Do you express it in your behavior with other people? How?

2. *What kinds of people or circumstances make you feel this way?*

3. *When was the last time you felt this way?* What were the circumstances? Who was present? Did your feeling have to do with that person, with someone else, or with the situation? Did your feeling have to do with a memory that was triggered by something that happened?

4. *When in your life did you have this feeling the most strongly?* Was it directed to any specific person? Who? How did you express the feeling at that time? How do you feel now as you recall it?

5. *Did the way you expressed your feeling at that time differ from the way you fantasized about it later?* If so, how did it differ?

6. *Does your feeling make you anxious?* If so, how do you experience that anxiety mentally and physically?

7. *Does your feeling involve anger?* Have you been so angry that you fantasized lashing out at someone? What did you fantasize? Did you ever think of someone you were angry with being out of the picture? Did you ever fantasize that person dying? How did he or she die? Do you have a mental image of that death? Is it violent?

8. *Does your feeling involve guilt or self-sabotage?* Do you sometimes feel so guilty that you think you don't deserve any happiness or any social life with other people? Have you ever fantasized yourself dying? What is the worst punishment that you can think of for yourself? Enumerate the reasons why you think you deserve such a punishment.

9. *Does your feeling involve pain or hurt?* Make a list of the things people do that hurt you. Put the list in order, from most hurtful to least hurtful. What is your reac-

tion to that hurt? How does that experience of being hurt make you view yourself? Do you feel a sense of devaluation? Is the low self-esteem connected only to the events and circumstances in which you were hurt or is it experienced in a more general way as a statement of who you are?

10. *Is your feeling connected most with any one person, past or present, living or dead?* Who is that person? How do you feel as you think about that person right now? What would you miss about that person if he or she were to die? If that person is dead, what do you miss about him or her? What are your feelings as you think about the things you would miss or do miss?

What would you say to that person if he or she were here now? How do you think the person would respond? What would that person say about you?

Take a few minutes to imagine a conversation in which you state your emotion (the "I feel..." with which you began the exercise) and the other person answers. In your mind, make the conversation continue for three or four minutes.

In your imagined conversation, were the opinions expressed totally negative or totally positive, or were both opinions present? Does the imaginary conversation make you feel any differently than when you started this exercise? Were there any surprises in the conversation that might help you get free of your troubling feeling?

11. *Think of three people in your current life with whom you might have real conversations about the emotion that is the subject of this self-exploration.* During the next week or two, seek those people out and have such conversations. Try to express your feelings honestly and to learn more about your feelings and those of the other person as the two of you talk.

You can use this self-exploration to examine many negative and troubling feelings. With repeated use, the exercise will yield increasingly beneficial results. If your initial reactions have not been all you think they should be, put the exercise aside and go over it again tomorrow; if you continue working with the exercise, your self-awareness will increase. You can use this same process whenever you're faced with a situation that generates an uncomfortable emotion.

CHAPTER 10

Mental Fitness

One of the universal issues that dominates human existence is the dilemma of passivity versus action. Intrinsic to the process of short-term therapy is activity on the part of the therapist, who prompts the patient to action.

For many decades the state of the therapeutic art has been based on intellectual abstractions and philosophical concepts. Psychoanalysis has been top-heavy with theory; it has lacked a technique that prompts the patient to take charge. Traditional therapy has fallen prey to the intellectual's disease, the idea that if we can just understand something, we will be all right.

Insight and understanding take us just so far, however. Clarification must become the springboard, the jumping-off point to taking charge of your life. To maintain mental fitness, you must demand from yourself a willingness to take action and be responsible. Once your defenses have

been clarified and broken through, once you have acknowledged and experienced emotionally the core issues in your
life, and once the obstacles to progress have been delineated, you then face that central question: What are you going
to do about it?

Some of the most valuable activity for emotional change
is not particularly dramatic. It involves forsaking the seduc-
tive roles we've discussed—wearing the mantle of guilt,
giving in to the allure of the victim role, being righteously
indignant. All of these modes of behavior are attractive;
they are the lazy way of dealing with a problem. It's easy to
be victimized, angry, indignant, to talk about what "they"
did.

It's not so easy to acknowledge that your unexamined
emotions have been detrimental to you and perhaps to
others, that you have had negative impulses, some that
you have acted on and some that you've kept inside
yourself. It's not so easy to take action, to forsake these
roles that were so appealing in the past, but it is much
more rewarding.

What are you going to do about it? This book has
succeeded if it has helped you realize that you must ask
yourself that question time and time again. Internalizing it
will increase your ability to accomplish for yourself the goals
you have set.

Intimacy: The Importance of Being Useful

Intimacy is an essential component in the process of
healing your painful and conflicted emotions and achieving
balance in your emotional life. Intimate experiences encourage empathy, understanding, and trust.

What do I mean by achieving intimacy? I mean allowing
people to be useful to you, having someone who is truly
supportive, allowing friends to be close, letting people see

your intimate thoughts and feelings, experiencing emotions and the events of life with other people—in a phrase, not going it alone. You can't have a satisfying life as an isolated human being.

For the longest time it was frowned on to show tears: women who cried were called hysterical, and men were branded weak, at best. If you have an emotion, why fight it back and not let another person see it? Everyone has had emotions that have made them tearful at some time. What is the premium on hiding those tears from others? The result is that you suffer a lot—and alone.

In the cooperative experience of intimacy, each person allows the other to be useful. Partners provide each other with important feedback. In any relationship—whether personal, professional, or just friendly—people commit themselves in every way that they can. When two people are intimate, they are not appendages of each other but resources; they help each other fill in the blanks that life so often presents. When one has insecurities and misperceptions, the other person validates what the two of them are sharing.

Between two people who are intimate, superficially supportive sentiments are not as helpful as statements that reflect what one of them is saying and feeling. For example, you might say, "When my father was dying, I was not there. I couldn't deal with his death. I avoided him, and that causes me a great deal of pain and guilt. I haven't liked myself since, and I can see that I've done things to sabotage myself." It's not useful for the other person to say, "Oh, it really wasn't that way. You didn't mean it. Your father knew you loved him." It would be more useful for the other person to acknowledge your feeling, to say, "This must be very difficult for you." That implies that your partner is on your wavelength and isn't avoiding the issue by telling you that everything's okay.

Achieving intimacy means having or finding another person who acknowledges your feelings and reflects them back to you. In the same way, a therapist's goal should be to help you get in touch with and clarify those feelings, rather than tell you that it wasn't a problem in the way you perceive it to be. You're not going to believe that anyway. The benefits of supportive statements in therapy last perhaps a few minutes—certainly no longer than it takes the patient to get to the street level or the parking lot. Whether it's in a personal relationship or with a therapist, the goal is to have somebody who can understand what you're suffering and be there to help you sort out your problems.

Living in Harmony with Your World

You constantly receive data from the outside world that you compute in ways that may be erroneous. This subtle but very real hurdle stands in the way of your achieving a sense of well-being, for your perceptions of other people and therefore your perceptions of yourself affect your ability to view yourself positively.

One of the most troublesome misperceptions that people fall prey to is the notion that we should strive for perfection. In our universe, perpetual motion machines and unicorns do not exist; neither does perfection. Yet we live under the sway of common, everyday delusions—that we can be perfect, that it's possible to avoid doing wrong, that we can escape guilt, that we can always make the correct choice, that we can be totally free of our past.

Living in harmony with your world implies that you have an appropriate view of the diverse elements in your life, that you understand that life contains both good and bad, that it's happy and it's sad. It implies that you do the best you can, that your expectations should be high but that they should also be realistic, that harboring unrealistic expectations is just another type of self-sabotage.

Achieving harmony in your world involves understanding who you are, what you can do, and what you can't do. It does not suggest that you "know your place." It does not suggest, "Don't think big." It implies developing an appropriate sense of yourself and placing an appropriate value on yourself—not a negative value, not a grandiose value, but a solid one.

A vitally important element of this process is the recognition that you are *striving* to maintain a standard. Sometimes you will fall short, but your shortcomings are natural and normal. It's like pedaling a bicycle: the ability to maintain 20 mph is something to work toward, but you won't always be able to do it.

We often have larger-than-life expectations of how we should behave in every instance, but the truth is that our attitudes and actions are not always exemplary. It's easy to assign consistently heroic characteristics to other people, to believe that they live on an elevated plane, but that's not life. On Monday a man runs into a burning building to rescue children. On Wednesday, in another set of circumstances, he walks away or stands by while somebody else does the rescuing or nobody does the rescuing.

Viewing personalities and behavior and emotions as static is like viewing the universe as static. By nature people are in a constant state of becoming, an evolution terminated only by death. There's an ebb and flow to our feelings, just as you may be up for a tennis game one day and win, and then lose to the same player the next day. Or you're the life of the party tonight, when your last time out you were a wallflower.

We tend to perceive the people around us as more consistent than that. We think that our heroes behave heroically every day, that they never suffer anxiety. The danger is that we operate under such illusions about people as we compare ourselves to those around us.

We're constantly taking readings about ourselves from our environment and other people, and as we do that we must be very careful, because our perception of what we observe is critical. If we believe that people are always the same—consistently heroic or consistently mundane and pedestrian—then we use that same standard in judging ourselves and thereby run the risk of constantly falling short and disappointing ourselves.

As we search for a sense of harmony, it's important to acknowledge our limitations, because in doing so we can direct our energy and productivity into areas where they will do the most good. For instance, most physicists don't spend a lot of time thinking about the universe before there was space and time, because that's unknowable. Being respectful of how far you can go in any field of endeavor or in any experience is conducive to greater rather than less satisfaction in life.

Knowing your limits is not a common prescription in our New Age environment. I'm not saying you should be happy with your lot in life if you're not. My point is that unless you know your limits, you can't stretch yourself to them and you can't go beyond where you are.

Finally, to live in harmony with your world (with the emphasis on *your* world), you need to have an inner direction, a navigational sextant by which you chart your course. You require a sense of inner direction in order to be satisfied with yourself, at peace with yourself. Other people don't have to comprehend it or even know about it.

When he wrote *Tropic of Cancer*, Henry Miller believed the book would never be published, yet he lived in impoverished circumstances for the sake of writing it. His inner direction sustained him and allowed him to do without things that most people would consider important and necessary. Miller was driven by a force that didn't involve the approval of the rest of the world.

Your inner direction can be an overall philosophy of what you want to do with your life. It also can be expressed as something more mundane: for example, that you want to complete a particular task before six o'clock tonight, a task you're doing for no reason but to satisfy yourself. It can incorporate both the broadest overview and the way you live day by day. It can be spiritual, philosophical, or practical, or all three.

Your internal direction finder, your personal navigational sextant, is purely subjective. It belongs to you alone, and it gets you through life. If you value the concepts presented in this book enough to carry them with you, the way they take shape in your life will help determine your sense of inner direction, for it's the part of you where psychiatric, philosophical, and spiritual issues converge.

Why Your Problems Never Go Away Completely

As you've undergone therapy or worked through this book, you may have fantasized about the moment when you would shout "Eureka!" and rush off into the sunset, cured of your ills and invulnerable to emotional turmoil and stress.

Within the therapeutic community, we sometimes hear about "total resolution of the neurotic state" and 100 percent cure rates. When these ideas are bandied about, I think of Kierkegaard, who reported that when he encountered philosophers who claimed they had found absolute truth, he would begin to spread his handkerchief in order to kneel before them, only to hear them say that perhaps their theory needed just a little more work.

Anyone who claims to know the truth is peddling snake oil. Likewise, conflicts are part of the existential condition.

We can no more totally eliminate them than we can view the universe from the outside looking in. Even when we have confronted and resolved our most difficult core issues, discomforts occasionally return. New situations provoke reactions that we had hoped to be rid of. Relationships continue to cause difficulty. There are stresses on the job. When we're faced with a loss, old reactions threaten us. Familiar anxieties haunt us.

In the Western world at the end of the twentieth century, people tend to believe that if we can just understand a problem we can solve it, and they want to know why therapy can't make our emotional problems go away completely. The reason is that the psyche is a repository for a spectrum of feelings and memories, some of which took place before we developed reason and the ability to use language—during the precognitive period. We cannot get back to that time and dismantle the emotional constructs that came together then.

The experiences of the precognitive period fall into one of two categories. In the first, the infant feels harmony, contentment, and a sense that it will continue to survive in a state of well-being. In the second, chaos and panic prevail, and the baby feels a primal terror of annihilation. Because of their intensity, these experiences become embedded as a core part of the psyche and constitute a partial source of our later difficulties. Yet that time remains beyond recall. It can't be understood and never will be. Various therapies, some unorthodox, attempt to get us back to the precognitive period, but that's not possible. Such therapies only project the memories and feelings of the present onto the early stages of life.

The part of our emotional life that is rooted in that unknowing and unknowable early period has always influenced us and will continue to do so throughout our lives. It is what is in control when, although we "know better," we keep repeating negative behavior.

This happens mainly in two ways. Because our earliest existence was dominated by two opposing emotional states— harmony and contentment as opposed to chaos and panic— we have within us a strong urge to understand issues in absolute terms. This urge emerges powerfully when we are faced with critical emotional situations, which we tend to see in black-and-white terms, with a sense of finality and irrevocability: "I'll never find anyone else" or "I'm doomed to failure if I lose this job."

Backing up this tendency to understand situations in all-or-nothing terms is our primal fear of the negative emotional state of that early time—a lack of nurturance and a resulting fear of annihilation. When a woman claims to have lost her sense of security—"My husband left me, I thought my life was over, and I didn't think I could go on"—she has tapped into an emotional dread of annihilation that originated in her precognitive past, a past she has difficulty dealing with because she cannot understand its true nature.

The existence of this early, unknowable period helps explain the anxiety and panic we feel when we are faced with certain emotional situations. In order to guarantee a satisfactory outcome and avoid an unacceptable one, we turn to the impulses and behaviors, ineffective though they may be, to which we have been conditioned instead of trusting the newer—that is, less proven—ways of reacting we have learned in therapy or through self-analysis. Because our desire for the precognitive sense of contentment— and our fear of its opposite—is so strong, we are afraid to trust any approach other than the one we have been conditioned to for so many years.

Within each of us, a precognitive emotional caldron churns concurrently with our superimposed adult reasoning nature that tries to make sense of it all. We can know that the caldron exists, but we lack the means to assess its contents. Our only assets are our cognitive powers, and they can't help us. The point is that we should not be trying to understand. We should accept the fact that we *cannot* understand.

"What good will this do?" ask the staunch believers in intellect. The answer is that we do not have to understand them completely to be able to deal with and attenuate our feelings.

Just as a swimmer must respect the ocean, we must respect our deep and intense feelings, the unknowable ones that originated in the precognitive period as well as the anger, guilt, and hurt that emerged during times that we can remember.

Respecting your psyche means understanding the need for constant vigilance, especially regarding the central issues that you uncover. They will always be with you, although you have minimized them. Even in quiet, undramatic periods of your life, they are likely to intrude on you as dreams, moods, "crazy" thoughts, and unexplainable feelings.

These occasional rumblings needn't frighten you. You should actually welcome them as reminders that you can't end your vigilance. Emotional well-being is an ongoing process, just like physical exercise.

Maintaining Mental Fitness

There are very few things in life that we accomplish and have automatic mastery over ever after. Swimming and riding a bicycle come to mind, but to do them really well practice and discipline are required.

We tend to view our accomplishments as static rather than in process. You go into therapy and experience a change in your awareness and behavior. Now you're "fixed." You've faced your worst fears, and don't have to worry about all that anymore.

This is the type of thinking that ruins the results of diets. You stick to a program for six months and lose the weight. Then you go back to your old ways of eating and gain it back. The foolishness of this approach is becoming more and more apparent, and people are starting to focus on changing the way they eat. As a culture we are coming to accept the idea that maintaining weight and physical fitness is a lifelong process.

In an interview Arnold Schwarzenegger was asked, "If you pump iron, when you stop doesn't all that mass turn to flab and fat?" He answered, "Why should you ever stop?" While most of us don't work out to the same extent Schwarzenegger does, his reply is an excellent one. Why would you want to stop eating right or exercising regularly? If you've discovered a new and a better way to live, why would you want to go back to the old way? Like physical conditioning, mental awareness is a continuing process. A person must be constantly on the lookout for the resurfacing of old, unacceptable patterns. A healthy mental outlook, like physical fitness, is hard work. It requires a commitment not only to change but to maintain that change.

You're embarking upon a new way of viewing yourself in the world. Over the years situations will occur—in small ways on an everyday basis, and in major ways as your life changes and as loved ones die—that will require emotional strength and resilience. As you face life's hardships, you must avoid behavior that is self-pitying, angry, guilty, isolating, and distancing. You must continue to work for a sense of worth and for usefulness, effectiveness, and the other good feelings that bring joy and meaning to life.

I hope that, having read this book, you have expanded your notions about therapy—what it can do and what it can't do—and have gained respect for those limitations, as well as recognizing that we all have the ability to enhance our lives. If you will think in appropriate terms about the human condition, you won't have to experience needless angst and frustration based on misperceptions not only of what is but of what will never be. When viewed within the proper context, the wishes and desires you cherish as you journey through life are do-able. Perhaps this book has helped in some way to make that journey more comprehensible.

Acknowledgments

To Paul Fargis of Stonesong Press, for standing by this book; to Sheree Bykofsky of Stonesong, for her editorial work; and to the editors at Warner Books: Leslie Keenan, Beth Lieberman, and Tracy Bernstein: thank you.

I'm indebted to several professional colleagues who read the manuscript and provided expert commentary: Sonia Austria, Ph.D.; Michael Alpert, M.D.; Michael Costanzo, M.D.; Arlene Feinblatt, M.D.; Steven Katz, M.D.; Roosey Khawly, M.D.; John Moore, M.D.; and Carl Sonder, M.D.

I must make special mention of those who contributed to my thinking about short-term therapy: my teachers Habib Davanloo, M.D., and David Malan, M.D., as well as James Mann, M.D., Peter Sifneos, M.D., and other researchers in the field.

Thanks for their valuable criticism, suggestions, and support go to Tom Andrews, William Arraez, Oona Chaplin, Jennifer Holbert, Norma Kamali, Elizabeth Racine, Mimi Torchin, Michael Weinstein, Peter Weller, and Elia Zois.

Finally, I am grateful to Pat Fogarty, who enabled me to maintain my focus and say all the things I wanted to say in a way that was clear and comprehensible, even to myself. No small task, that.

Bibliography

Alexander, F., and T. M. French. *Psychoanalytic Therapy: Principles and Applications.* New York: Ronald Press, 1946.

Armstrong, S. "Dual Focus in Brief Psychodynamic Psychotherapy." *Psychotherapy and Psychosomatics* 33(1980): 147–54.

Balint, M., P. Ornstein, and E. Balint. *Focal Psychotherapy: An Example of Applied Psychoanalysis.* London: Tavistock, 1972.

Barten, H. H. "The Coming of Age of the Brief Psychotherapies." In *Progress in Community Health,* edited by L. Bellak and H. H. Barten. New York: Grune & Stratton, 1969.

Bellak, L., and L. Small. *Emergency Psychotherapy and Brief Psychotherapy.* New York: Grune & Stratton, 1978.

Budman, S. H., ed. *Forms of Brief Therapy.* New York: Guilford Press, 1981.

Budman, S. H., and A. S. Gurman. "The Practice of Brief Therapy." *Professional Psychology: Research and Practice* 14 (1983): 277–92.

Butcher, J. N., and M. P. Koss. "Research on Brief and Crisis-oriented Psychotherapies." In *Handbook of Psychotherapy and Behavior Change*, 2d ed., edited by S. L. Garfield and A. E. Bergin. New York: John Wiley, 1978.

Castelnuovo-Tedesco, P. "Brief Psychotherapy." In *American Handbook of Psychiatry*, 2d ed., Vol. 5, edited by S. Arieti. New York: Basic Books, 1975.

Davanloo, H., ed. *Basic Principles and Techniques in Short-term Dynamic Psychotherapy*. New York: Spectrum, 1978.

———, ed. *Short-term Dynamic Psychotherapy*. New York: Jason Aronson, 1980.

Firestein, S. *Termination in Psychoanalysis*. New York: International Universities Press, 1978.

Frank, J. D. *Persuasion and Healing*, 2d ed. Baltimore: Johns Hopkins University Press, 1973.

Frank, J. D., R. Hoehn-Saric, S. D. Imber, B. L. Liberman, and A. R. Stone. *Effective Ingredients of Successful Psychotherapy*. New York: Brunner/Mazel, 1978.

Freud, A., *The Ego and the Mechanisms of Defense*. London: Hogarth Press, 1936.

Freud, S., "Analysis Terminable and Interminable." In *Standard Edition of the Complete Psychological Works of Sigmund Freud*. Vol. 23. London: Hogarth Press, 1937, pp. 216–53.

Gill, M. M. *Analysis of Transference I: Theory and Technique*. New York: International Universities Press, 1982.

Gustafson, J. P. "The Complex Secret of Brief Psychotherapy in the Work of Malan and Balint." In *Forms of Brief Therapy*, edited by S. H. Budman. New York: Guilford Press, 1981.

Kernberg, O. F.. *Borderline Conditions and Pathological Narcissism*. New York: Jason Aronson, 1975.

———. *Object Relations Theory and Clinical Psychoanalysis*. New York: Jason Aronson, 1976.

Kohut, H. *The Search for the Self*. New York: International Universities Press, 1978.

Laing, R. D. *Knots*. New York: Pantheon, 1970.

Mahler, M. S., F. Pine, and A. Bergman. *The Psychological Birth of the Human Infant*. London: Hutchinson, 1975.

Malan, D. H., *A Study of Brief Psychotherapy.* New York: Plenum Press, 1963.

——. *The Frontier of Brief Psychotherapy.* New York: Plenum Press, 1976.

——. *Toward the Validation of Dynamic Psychotherapy: A Replication.* New York: Plenum Press, 1976.

——. *Individual Psychotherapy and the Science of Psychodynamics.* London: Butterworth, 1979.

Mann, J. *Time-Limited Psychotherapy.* Cambridge, Mass.: Harvard University Press, 1973.

Mann, J., and R. Goldman. *A Casebook in Time-limited Psychotherapy.* New York: McGraw-Hill, 1982.

Menninger, K. *Theory of Psychoanalytic Technique.* New York: Basic Books, 1958.

Reich, W. *Character Analysis.* Translated by T. Wocfus. Rangeley, Me.: Orgonics Institute Press, 1933.

Ryle, A. "The Focus in Brief Interpretive Psychotherapy: Dilemmas, Traps, and Snags." *British Journal of Psychiatry* 134 (1979): 46–54.

Sachs, J. S., "Negative Factors in Brief Psychotherapy: An Empirical Assessment." *Journal of Consulting and Clinical Psychology* 51 (1983): 557–64.

Sifneos, P. E., *Short-term Psychotherapy and Emotional Crisis.* Cambridge, Mass.: Harvard University Press, 1972.

——. *Short-term Dynamic Psychotherapy: Evaluation and Technique.* New York: Plenum Press, 1979.

Small, L. *The Briefer Psychotherapies.* 2d ed. New York: Brunner/ Mazel, 1979.

Stierlin, H. "Short-term versus Long-term Psychotherapy in Light of a General Theory of Human Relationships." *British Journal of Psychiatry* 32 (1968):127–35.

Wolberg, L. *Handbook of Short-term Psychotherapy.* New York: Grune & Stratton, 1980.